modern concepts
of internal auditing series

Auditor Independence and Systems Design

by Larry E. Rittenberg

Published by
The Institute of Internal Auditors
International Headquarters
249 Maitland Avenue
Altamonte Springs, Florida 32701

ISBN 0-89413-053-6
Library of Congress Catalog Card Number 77-79366

FOREWORD

Internal auditing is an independent appraisal activity within an organization for reviewing operations as a service to management. The important word here is *independent.* Properly established, internal auditing is the focal point for examining all organizational controls. Today's internal auditors must constantly reevaluate their role in relationship to organizational changes if they are to accomplish the objectives of internal auditing.

One such change is the participation of internal auditors in the EDP design phase. This report provides an analysis of the effect internal audit participation in EDP design has on the internal auditor's independence.

The study concludes that the independence issue should not deter internal auditors from performing design-phase audits. On the contrary, research indicates that internal auditors can make important design-phase contributions to an organization without impairing their independence.

The research points out, however, that auditors must be constantly aware of potential threats to independence. This report identifies a number of areas where managers have the ability to take actions to avoid any loss of independence due to EDP design-phase auditing.

The "research highlights" section introduces many major findings of the study. Each of these is developed in detail in the following seven sections of the report.

The Institute of Internal Auditors expresses its sincere appreciation to the 41 organizations and approximately 200 individuals who took part in this study. We also thank the International EDP Auditing Committee for its contribution.

James R. Kelly, CIA
International President

ABOUT THE AUTHOR

Larry E. Rittenberg is an assistant professor of accounting and information systems at the University of Wisconsin — Madison. He lectures primarily in the fields of auditing (including computer auditing), financial accounting, and management information systems. He holds a PhD in accounting from the University of Minnesota and a BA and MBA from Michigan State University. Dr. Rittenberg, an active member of The Institute of Internal Auditors, has served on many chapter-level committees and is currently a member of the International Education Committee. He is a CPA and a member of the American Institute of Certified Public Accountants and the American Accounting Association.

ACKNOWLEDGMENTS

Many individuals contributed to this study. Indeed, the research could not have been accomplished without the cooperation of those many internal auditors and other individuals who willingly spent their time completing the research questionnaires. Their cooperation is gratefully acknowledged.

The research was conducted as part of the requirements for a PhD degree from the University of Minnesota. Many members of the accounting faculty at the university contributed to the final product. Professor Charles Purdy, chairman of the thesis committee, provided numerous suggestions and constructive criticism throughout the entire project.

Professor Gordon Davis suggested the need for the research and was very helpful in identifying the companies which participated in the study. In addition, his comments regarding the questionnaires and manuscript were most helpful.

Professor Michael Barrett provided substantial suggestions on the research design. The help of these three professors is gratefully acknowledged.

I would also like to thank the numerous reviewers of earlier drafts for their many suggestions. In particular, I would like to thank Chuck Litecky, a colleague at the University of Wisconsin — Madison, for his input.

I would like to thank the many members of The Institute of Internal Auditors who helped in identifying companies active in EDP auditing and the International EDP Auditing Committee for its support of the project. In particular, I am grateful for the help, encouragement, comments, and support given by William E. Perry, CIA, director of EDP and research for The Institute, and the help rendered by Kenneth H. Meuwissen, CIA, chairman of the research committee of IIA's Twin Cities Chapter. Finally, I would like to acknowledge the project support and funding by the Twin Cities Chapter of IIA, the Northwest Bancorporation, the First Bank System, and the Burlington Northern Corporation.

Larry E. Rittenberg, PhD, CPA

INTERNATIONAL EDP AUDITING COMMITTEE 1976-77

F. B. Palmer, CIA, Chairman
Colgate-Palmolive Company
Emerson, New Jersey

Tom Baldwin
The Williams Companies
Tulsa, Oklahoma

Jack P. Colgan
Lockheed-Georgia Company
Marietta, Georgia

Roy C. Culbertson, CIA
Pacific Gas & Electric Company
San Francisco, California

R. H. Dively, CIA
The BFGoodrich Company
Akron, Ohio

Edward A. Evans, CIA
Unilever, Ltd.
Port Sunlight, Cheshire, England

T. J. Geldon
Western Bancorp Data
Processing Company
Reno, Nevada

Willard E. Hick
Massachusetts Mutual Life
Insurance Company
Springfield, Massachusetts

Everett C. Johnson
Haskins & Sells
Los Angeles, California

S. B. MacNab
Bell Canada
Montreal, Quebec, Canada

William C. Mair
Touche Ross & Co.
Detroit, Michigan

John Nuxall
Peat, Marwick, Mitchell & Co.
New York, New York

G. I. R. Pawley
Shell International Petroleum
Company, Ltd.
Winchester, Hampshire, England

Kenneth A. Pollock
U.S. General Accounting Office
Washington, D. C.

Walter D. Pugh
Price Waterhouse & Co.
New York, New York

Richard A. Ress
Shell Oil Company
Houston, Texas

Roy G. Saltman
National Bureau of Standards
Washington, D. C.

Harold Weiss, CIA
Automation Training Center, Inc.
Reston, Virginia

John J. Workman
U.S. Steel Corporation
Pittsburgh, Pennsylvania

Joseph J. Wasserman, CIA
Consultant
West Orange, New Jersey

P. J. Corum
Bank of Montreal
Montreal, Quebec, Canada

Warren Nogle, CIA, CPA
Finance America Corporation
Allentown, Pennsylvania

Clifford A. Stevens
Harter Bank and Trust Company
Canton, Ohio

David R. Fisher, CPA, PE
American Savings Association
Southfield, Michigan

Carmen Spinelli
J. K. Lasser & Company
New York, New York

Marvin Stille
The Marine Corporation
Milwaukee, Wisconsin

Phyllis Thompson
Genesee Bank
Flint, Michigan

Kent Yarnall
Touche Ross & Co.
New York, New York

Bob Leard
U.S. Department of Agriculture
San Francisco, California

Aldo Neim
Clarkson, Gordon & Company
Toronto, Ontario, Canada

Frank J. Gaffney
Xerox Corporation
Rochester, New York

CONTENTS

TABLES

FIGURES

1 | INTRODUCTION

Data processing systems have become an integral part of most organizations during the past decade. As organizations become more dependent on data processing, they also become more vulnerable to computer-related losses. Terms such as "computer fraud" and "data security" have been added to our vocabulary as evidence of the risks associated with complex data processing systems.

Management and others now recognize the need for an independent evaluation of data processing controls. In many organizations this has resulted in requests for internal auditors to do more "computer auditing." This, traditionally, means more reviews and tests of existing EDP applications and evaluations of data security. Many, however, feel the auditor's function should be more *preventive* than *detective* and urge internal auditors to become involved during the design phase of new EDP applications, reviewing controls at a point where changes can be made economically.

Design-phase auditing creates a dilemma in the minds of many internal auditors.They fear that involvement during the design phase of new EDP applications may impair their independence. Since independence is considered essential to the effectiveness of the internal auditor,[1] there is considerable debate about the advisability of internal audit design-phase activity.

This report presents the results of a major study of the effects of EDP design-phase auditing on perceptions of internal audit independence. A combination of questionnaires, hypothetical case situations, and interviews were utilized to assess various aspects of the design-phase independence issue as perceived by internal auditors and by those who rely on, or react to, internal audit reports in the field of EDP. Almost 200 individuals from 41 large organizations took part in the study. The participating organizations represent a wide range of EDP audit experience. Approximately one-half of the internal auditors had little or no EDP design-phase audit experience, whereas the other half had considerable EDP design-phase audit experience.

[1] The Institute of Internal Auditors, *Statement of Responsibilities of Internal Auditors* (Orlando, Florida), 1976.

Although the research was conducted in the specific area of EDP auditing, many of the findings are applicable to other audit areas wherein auditors perform follow-up audits to review the disposition of previous audit recommendations. The remainder of this report provides a detailed description of the research process, findings, an analysis of current EDP audit activities, and some recommendations for the internal audit profession.

2 | RESEARCH HIGHLIGHTS

In recent years, there has been considerable debate about whether internal auditors should become involved during the design phase of new EDP applications or information systems development. The proponents of such participation advocate a *preventive* approach to computer auditing. They feel design-phase auditing contributes to an organization by insuring that needed controls are built into new systems and that a new system will be auditable.

The opposing viewpoint questions design-phase audit participation for fear that such participation may impair the auditor's independence. Because independence is considered essential to internal auditing, opponents question the wisdom of audit approaches which jeopardize independence.

This report presents the results of a study which addresses the issue of design-phase auditing and independence in 41 large organizations. Data on design-phase auditing and independence were gathered from internal auditors, CPA's, heads of Data Processing departments, and members of top management. Companies participating in the study included both those with very little EDP audit experience and those with considerable EDP audit experience.

This study does not directly address the issue of whether design-phase audits are more important than postinstallation audits. Rather, the study focuses on:

- The various approaches to EDP design-phase auditing
- Structure and policies of Internal Audit departments regarding design-phase auditing
- Personal characteristics and competence of individual auditors
- How each of these factors affects the ability of an auditor (or Internal Audit Department) to perform EDP design-phase audits and later independently audit the developed application

MAJOR FINDINGS

The research identifies a number of areas where internal audit managers have the ability to influence, or take actions to minimize, the loss of independence due to design-phase auditing. Here are some of the major findings which this report discusses later in more detail.

There is considerable agreement among the study participants on the factors affecting internal audit independence and the objectives of EDP auditing.

The auditor's technical EDP competence is an important influence on perceptions of independence.

Design-phase audit activities can be divided into three groups. Activities in two of these groups (reviewing for adequacy of application controls and performing compliance tests of general controls) generally do not impair perceptions of audit independence, whereas activities in the third group (auditors participating in the design process) greatly reduce perceptions of audit independence.

Assigning different auditors to design activities and post-installation audits was perceived to be unnecessary when development activities were reviewed for compliance with company procedures. Such assignments were thought to be effective in increasing independence when application controls were reviewed but ineffective when internal auditors were active designers.

The Internal Audit Department can be structured to achieve maximum independence through supervision and review of work, assigning auditors to tasks, and so forth.

Many EDP design-phase audit activities now performed by internal auditors are not viewed as prejudicial to audit independence.

Organizational factors such as top management support are important in promoting an environment of maximum independence for internal auditors.

STUDY RECOMMENDATIONS

Recommendations stemming from the study are:

Internal auditors should be involved in the design phase but only in reviewing, testing, and assessing the adequacy of application controls and in reviewing the adequacy and compliance with general controls over the application development process.

Internal auditors should increase their EDP technical competence.

Top management support for internal audit activities should be developed as one means of increasing independence.

The Internal Audit Department should be structured for maximum independence through supervision and review of work, assignment of auditors to tasks, auditors' sign-off, adherence to IIA's *Code of Ethics of Internal Auditors,* and other practices.

It is recommended that a separate EDP audit section be established in large organizations. These EDP audit sections should perform design-phase audit activities and, when possible, coordinate postinstallation audits with other members of the internal audit staff.

In small organizations, at least one auditor should be an EDP audit specialist and the remaining auditors should be capable of conducting postinstallation audits.

3 THE NATURE OF EDP DESIGN-PHASE AUDITS

IMPORTANCE OF DESIGN-PHASE AUDITING

The increased complexity of new EDP developments leads to the question, should internal auditors limit their audit activities to systems already installed? Indeed, there is some feeling that special problems associated with newer, more complex EDP systems leave auditors with little choice but to become involved early in the system's development. For example, Keyes states:

> *It is no longer feasible from practical and economical viewpoints to review systems after they have been completed. . .In my opinion, there is but one conclusion: The auditor must play a role in systems development if he is going to fulfill his obligation to management. If this is not done, he may be working in an environment which has less than sufficient controls (and) is difficult or impossible to audit. . .*[2]

Other advocates of design-phase auditing present the following arguments for design-phase audit participation:[3]

- Effective controls should be designed into the system because of the often *prohibitive cost* of adding them later.
- Assurance is needed for *adequate security and backup* facilities to protect valuable data.
- Internal audit review of control adequacy during systems design may *influence the scope of the CPA's audit.*
- Internal auditors may be the best persons to develop and employ detection techniques which may *deter fraud.*
- Internal audit review is necessary to assure audit trails and future auditability of major on-line systems.

Most arguments for design-phase audit participation can be summarized in four major categories:

---

[2] Edward G. Keyes, "The Auditor's Role in New Systems Development," *The Internal Auditor* (January-February, 1972), p. 32.

[3] See particularly the articles by Canning, Keyes, and Pauley and the books by Jancura and Touche Ross & Co. listed in the bibliography.

Need for a control perspective: Internal auditors are control specialists. As representatives of management, auditors can add a managerial perspective to new system developments. Also, it is more economical to install controls during development.

Cost of developing new systems: Cost overruns on system development are the rule, not the exception. Many developed systems do not accomplish projected benefits. Internal auditors can audit for compliance with established controls and critique the system development process, leading to improved control over the system development process.

Complex systems: The newer, more complex systems, such as those supported by data-base management systems, require more preventive approaches to auditing. This requires design-phase consideration of alternatives. Another example is the development of *electronic funds transfer systems,* where an audit perspective is needed to insure that all critical aspects are considered.

Positive view by management and external auditors: A separate part of this research sought top management's and CPAs' views of the importance of various EDP audit objectives. Both groups viewed design-phase audit activities as highly important.

Up to this point, design-phase auditing has been referred to in general terms only. However, as seen in the various arguments for design-phase auditing, there is considerable variation in the scope and nature of design-phase audit activities. It is possible that some design audit activities influence audit independence, whereas others do not. Thus, it is necessary to define "design-phase auditing" more precisely.

TYPES OF DESIGN-PHASE AUDITS

Three basic EDP audit concepts are necessary to understand potential differences in EDP design-phase audits: the nature of EDP controls reviewed, the concept of a "systems life cycle" or "EDP application life cycle," and the audit orientation or audit approach implied in IIA's *Statement of Responsibilities of Internal Auditors.*

Types of Controls Reviewed

The Auditing Standards Executive Committee of the American Institute of Certified Public Accountants clarified auditing terminology in its *SAS No. 3* by distinguishing between "application controls" and "general controls" in EDP environments as follows:

> *Application Controls:* Controls related to specific tasks performed by EDP. Their function is to provide reasonable assurance that the recording, processing, and reporting of data are properly performed. There is considerable choice in the particular procedures and records used to effect application controls. Application controls are often

categorized as "input controls," "processing controls," and "output controls."

> *General Controls:* (a) The plan of organization and operation of the EDP activity; (b) the procedures for documenting, reviewing, testing, and approving systems or programs and changes thereto; (c) controls built into the equipment by the manufacturer; (d) controls over access to equipment and data files; and (e) other data and procedural controls affecting overall operations. *Weaknesses in general controls often have pervasive effects.*[4] (Italics added)

An EDP application is a specific function performed by a computer program(s). Examples of EDP applications are payroll, inventory record keeping, and market sales analysis programs. Thus, a design-phase audit of *application controls* focuses on the adequacy of application controls built into the new application.

General controls include the standards and procedures that specify how things are done in EDP. For example, there should be documentation and testing standards for new EDP development projects as well as defined procedures to ensure user and audit reviews. A design-phase audit of *general controls* might address either their effectiveness as prescribed for new EDP development or the compliance of actual design procedures with those prescribed.

The Relationship of the EDP Application Life Cycle to Design-Phase Audits

The basic idea of an application life cycle is that every (EDP) application must go through essentially the same process as it is conceived, developed, and implemented. The stages in the life cycle provide a basis for planning and control, which is a basis for viewing the auditor's potential involvement with an application.

There are numerous concepts about an application life cycle. Most major application development includes the major phases depicted in Figure 1. The content and length of each stage will likely vary by organization and the complexity of the system under development. The first five phases of the life cycle are referred to as the "design phase" and the last two as the "postinstallation phase."

From an audit standpoint, each phase has distinct risks and audit concerns. Management risks and audit concerns associated with each phase of the life cycle are identified in Figure 2. These risks are linked, in turn, to the type of control (general or application) that addresses the area of concern. Thus, it can be seen that the auditor's auditing philosophy and control orientation will influence potential EDP audit involvement. Although some internal auditors focus their attention on application controls, the need for an assessment and review of general control development is becoming widely recognized.

---

[4] American Institute of Certified Public Accountants, *Statement on Auditing Standards No. 3: The Effects of EDP on the Auditor's Study and Evaluation of Internal Control* (New York: AICPA, 1974), p. 3.

Figure 1
EDP Application Life Cycle

Phases of Life Cycle	Major Activities of Each Phase
Design Phases	
1. Feasibility Assessment	Develop project proposal Prepare cost/benefit study Decide whether to proceed with the system Prepare time and cost budgets
2. Information Analysis	Determine information requirements for new system
3. System Analysis and Design	Develop system and program specifications Determine equipment requirements Make equipment decision if necessary Further define user needs Define security and audit needs
4. Procedure and Program Development	Code and debug programs Develop user manuals Develop processing manuals
5. Testing and Conversion	Test the system Transfer processing to new system Educate users
Postinstallation Phases	
6. Operation and Maintenance	Modify as necessary Maintain ongoing operations
7. Postaudit	Critically review system accomplishments in terms of time, cost, benefits, and user satisfaction Recommend improvements for future developments

Source: Gordon B. Davis, *Management Information Systems: Conceptual Foundations, Structure and Development* (New York: McGraw-Hill Book Company, 1974), pp. 413-420. For alternative formulations of a system's life cycle, see Glans, *et al., Management Systems;* Hartman, *et al., Management Information Systems Handbook;* and Shaw and Atkins, *Managing Computer Systems Projects.*

Figure 2
Internal Audit Within an EDP Application Life Cycle

Phase of EDP Application Life Cycle	Management Risks and Auditor Concerns	Type of Controls Addressing Risk
Design Phases		
1. Feasibility Assessment	Risk of committing resources to an improperly formulated proposal Highest risk of application failure occurs at this point	General
2. Information Analysis	Risk of developing a system that is not fitted to user needs Risk of conceptually developing a system which is physically inoperable One of the two highest areas of cost incurrence	General
3. System Analysis and Design	Risk of ignoring needed processing controls Risk of poor design from operating standpoint	Application General
4. Procedure and Program Development	Risk of ignoring controls to be built into the programs and for processing outside of computer Risk of cost overrun	Application General

5. Testing and Conversion	Risk of not fully testing controls Risk of implementing new system before all components are ready	Application General
Postinstallation Phases		
6. Operation and Maintenance	Inadequate security provisions Improper, incomplete, or inadequate processing of data Inadequate liaison with users and input personnel Inefficient usage of data processing resource	Application General
7. Postaudit	System does not achieve objectives, and there is little chance for change	General

The Influence of Audit Orientation On Design-Phase Audits

The scope and nature of design-phase audit activities will be influenced by the audit orientation adopted. IIA's *Statement of Responsibilities of Internal Auditors* gives the following as examples of audit activities:

■ Reviewing and appraising the soundness, adequacy, and application of accounting, financial, and other operating controls, and promoting effective control at reasonable cost.

■ Ascertaining the extent of compliance with established policies, plans, and procedures.

■ Ascertaining the extent to which company assets are accounted for and safeguarded from losses of all kinds.

■ Ascertaining the reliability of management data developed within the organization.

■ Appraising the quality of performance in carrying out assigned responsibilities.

■ Recommending operating improvements.

The first four activities represent the auditor's traditional approach of reviewing and testing accounting and managerial controls. The last two activities listed represent a potential expansion of audit activities into consulting. Since internal auditing applies to all managerial controls, the activities represented apply to either application or general controls surrounding EDP. Four categories of EDP design-phase audit activities suggested by the *Statement* include: audits of the adequacy and soundness of application controls, audit of systems design process for compliance with general controls, audit assistance by providing expert consultive recommendations relating to control aspects of new EDP developments, and audit participation as a member in various design activities by recommending improvements.

The differences in levels of design-phase audit involvement may be at least as influential upon perceptions of audit independence as the actual participation by auditors during the design phase (without specifying the exact participation).

A FRAMEWORK FOR VIEWING POTENTIAL CONFLICTS ASSOCIATED WITH DESIGN-PHASE AUDITING

A framework for viewing the internal auditor's potential audits of EDP applications may be developed along control and timing dimensions as follows:[5]

[5] Note that this framework is limited to EDP applications. In practice, internal auditors will also devote considerable time on audits of the total data processing center which might include an analysis of data security and procedures related to the ongoing activities of the data processing center.

Control orientation — Application controls / General controls

Timing — Design phase / Postinstallation phase

This framework highlighting potential conflicts that may impact audit independence is presented in Figure 3. The two postinstallation audits of EDP applications are:

Application controls audit: the evaluation and testing of the adequacy of EDP application controls in operation.

Operational postaudit of application development: the independent review and analysis of an implemented EDP application with emphasis on application accomplishments compared with costs and objectives.[6]

Figure 3
Framework for Internal Audit of EDP Applications

	Postinstallation Audits	
Design-Phase Audit Involvement	**Application Controls Audits**	**Operational Postaudit of Application Development**
Application control review	A	B
Operational audit of general controls surrounding application development	C	D

The two design-phase audits are:

Application control review: a review of the adequacy of controls designed into new EDP developments. Of particular interest are input, processing, and output controls. The controls may be embedded in the application software or included as procedures for handling input or output of data.

Operational audit of general controls surrounding application development: the review of application development procedures

[6] For a further discussion of this type of audit, see Harold Sollenberger and Alvin Arens, "Systems Control and the Post-Completion Systems Audit," *The Internal Auditor,* (March-April, 1973), pp. 22-33; and Gordon B. Davis, *Computer Data Processing* (New York, McGraw-Hill Book Company, 2nd ed., 1974), p. 204.

and documentation. Auditors are primarily concerned with the effectiveness and compliance with general controls over new EDP developments.

Internal audit independence may be impaired whenever auditors perform both design-phase and postinstallation audits of the same application. However, the potential conflicts in cells *A* (application control audits) and *D* (operational audits) of Figure 3 receive the most attention and constitute the primary focus of this research. In addition to the types of audits, the level of audit involvement will also be considered in determining the potential loss due to design-phase auditing. Figures 4 and 5 summarize audit activities for design-phase and postinstallation audits of cells *A* and *D* of Figure 3. The activities outlined in these two figures serve as a basis for an investigation of audit activities that may impair internal audit independence.

Figure 4

Audit Activities Applicable to Cell A: Design-Phase and Postinstallation Audits of Application Controls*

Application Control Audit Concern	Design-Phase Audit Activities: Application Control Review	Postinstallation EDP Application Audit Activities
Adequacy of application built into application Actual existence of application controls in operation	A. *Audit review for existence and adequacy of controls* Review for adequacy of controls; make recommendations. Review test procedures. Review adequacy of security and issue a report. Review design-phase development documentation for completeness. Review processing and user manuals. Issue letters of comment at end of each major phase. B. *Audit activities as a designer or consultant* Define or specify audit requirements. Participate in conversion tests of developing application. Prepare control documentation manual. Prepare audit guide.	A. *Review* Obtain information about application and procedures. B. *Testing* Ascertain that procedures and processes were performed correctly and by proper personnel. C. *Evaluation* Types of errors that could occur. Processing weaknesses. Security. Adequacy and effectiveness of application controls.

*These audit activities are illustrative only and do not contain all audit activities that could fit under this categorization.

Figure 5
Comparison of Audit Activities Applicable to Cell D: Design-Phase and Postinstallation Operational Audits of General Controls*

General Control Audit Concerns	Design-Phase *Operational Audit of General Controls Surrounding Application Development*	Postinstallation *Operational Postaudit of EDP Application Development*
Cost effectiveness	Review the reasonableness of cost-benefit analysis prepared during the feasibility study. Sign approval document noting auditor's assessment of the reasonableness of the estimates.	Compare actual costs with estimated costs and perceived benefits with estimated benefits.
Attainment of objectives	Appraise appropriateness of application during the feasibility study. Review and assess reasonableness of expected benefits. Evaluate potential risk. Act as a liaison between programmers, system designers, and users.	Assess the attainment of objectives including such things as: Timeliness of reports Completeness of reports Error limits Processing requirements Operating efficiency User satisfaction
Evaluation of application design procedures	Ascertain compliance of activities with prescribed standards and procedures. Sign approval document at completion of each stage.	Perform an objective review of system-design procedures. Evaluate personnel.

*These audit activities are illustrative only and do not contain all audit activities that could fit under this categorization.

4 INDEPENDENCE AND DESIGN-PHASE AUDITING

IMPORTANCE OF INTERNAL AUDIT INDEPENDENCE

The importance of independence is recognized in the definition of internal auditing:

> Internal auditing is an *independent appraisal* activity within an organization for the review of operations[7] (emphasis added).

Independence serves three essential purposes for internal auditors:[8]

■ It provides *auditor freedom* to determine audit programs, modes of investigations, and contents of audit reports (investigative freedom).

■ It promotes *audit objectivity.* This objectivity is needed in establishing audit criteria, opinions, and priorities (individual impartiality).

■ It *facilitates effective communication* of audit findings. An auditor perceived to be independent has greater creditability than one not perceived to be independent.

An auditor's independence is referred to as *real independence.* Real independence is to some degree a state of mind, and is thus difficult to measure. Each auditor, therefore, must perceive independence in his or her own way. *Perceived independence* refers to an individual's view of audit independence. This view may be based on observation of auditor activities, and may or may not be representative of the actual state of audit independence. However, since individuals act on their perceptions, auditors must be concerned with both real and perceived independence.

Investigative freedom and individual impartiality imply that a concept of internal audit independence must contain both an organizational and an individual component. Likewise, the

---

[7] *Statement of Responsibilities of Internal Auditors.*

[8] For a fuller discussion, see Robert Mautz and Hussein Sharaf, *The Philosophy of Auditing* (American Accounting Association, 1961).

Statement of Responsibilities of Internal Auditors recognizes both an organizational component (status within the organization) and an individual component (objectivity) in its discussion of internal audit independence. In addition, both the AICPA[9] and the comptroller general of the United States[10] have developed guidelines for audit independence that include both organizational relationships and individual factors.

A MODEL OF INTERNAL AUDIT INDEPENDENCE

As a basis for understanding the potential impact of design-phase auditing, a model of internal audit independence is developed and presented in Figure 6. The model shows that internal audit independence has both an organizational and an individual component, each consisting of a number of factors.

The organizational component affects the environment in which the internal auditor functions. This factor may significantly affect the auditor's freedom to perform activities and may also exert pressures either conducive or nonconducive to independent auditor actions.

The individual component consists of the individual auditor's state of mind and other influences that may affect the auditor's actions. The auditor's mental state represents psychological factors that affect the auditor's ability to think and act independently. Moreover, individuals have different independence traits. The other influences listed under individual independence show that more than a mental state is involved and that, even though an auditor may reach independent conclusions, there may be other factors that affect the auditor's actions. The Internal Audit Department may be able to control some of these influences and affect behavior by rewarding or constraining audit actions.

Design-phase auditing is put into perspective as one of the factors controllable by the Internal Audit Department. The nature and scope of design-phase auditing, as well as the manner in which auditors are assigned to tasks, is noted and classified in the model (Figure 6).

The remaining factors in the model may interact with design-phase auditing to produce results different from those obtained if each factor were viewed in isolation. In addition to drawing the distinction between the individual mental-state component and other influences on independence, the model offers the following conceptual advantages:

[9] John L. Carey and William O. Doherty, *Ethical Standards of the Accounting Profession* (New York: AICPA, 1966).

[10] The comptroller general of the United States, *Standards for Audit of Governmental Organizations, Programs, Activities, and Functions* (Washington, D. C.: U.S. Government Printing Office, 1972), pp. 16-18.

Figure 6
A Model of Internal Audit Independence

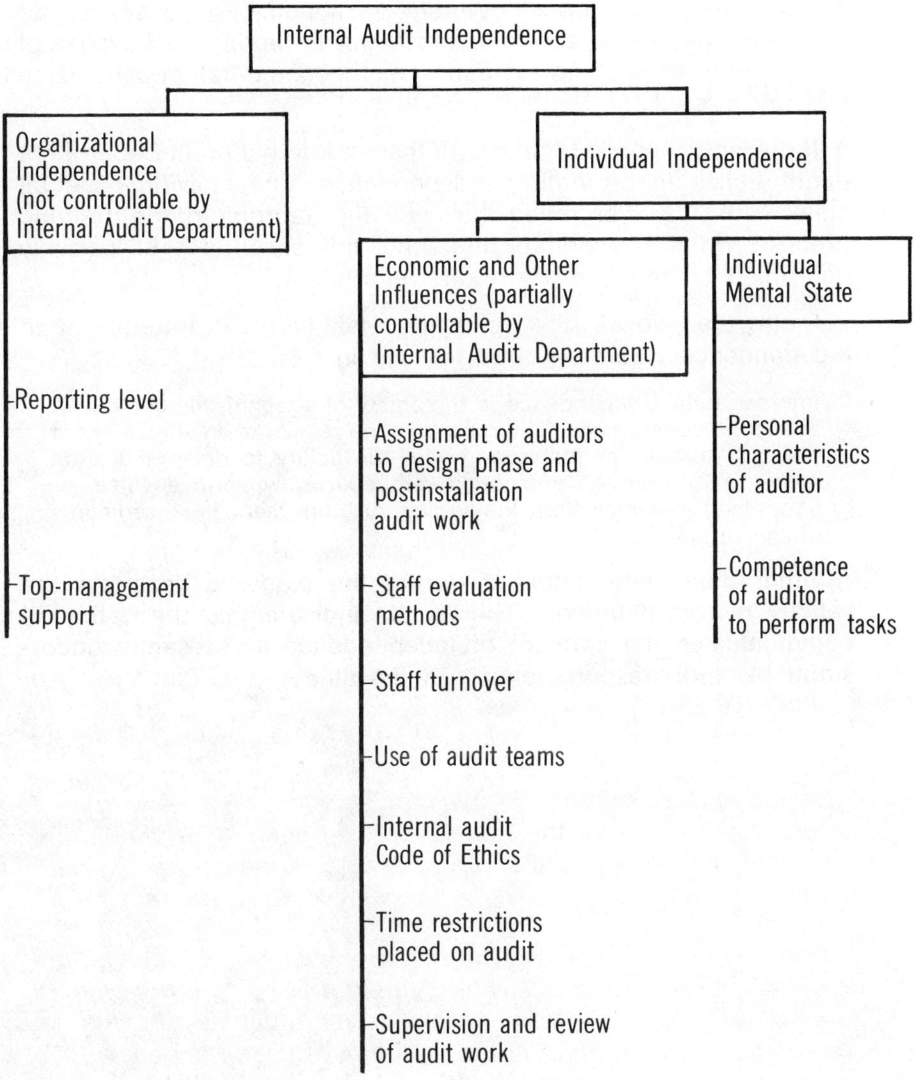

■ It recognizes the difficulties in discerning an individual's independent mental state.

■ It recognizes that, although an individual has the ability to think and act independently, he or she may not always respond with an independently developed opinion or action. For example, an individual may reach a conclusion about an audit; but because of other pressures such as evaluation methods, a different conclusion may be offered.

■ It presents a control framework that an Internal Audit Department might utilize in promoting independence. The individual mental state might be controlled through the recruiting and training process, whereas economy and other influences may be partially controlled by the Internal Audit Department.

From the model, the following definition of internal audit independence was developed for use in this study:

> Internal audit independence is the ability of a technically competent auditor to conduct and fully report on the results of an audit without personal bias or prejudice and with the ability to determine audit areas, audit scope, and audit procedures without adverse or controlling influence from the auditee or other managerial segments of the organization.

Other data were gathered during the study to ascertain the validity of this definition. The results indicate that the definition communicates the concept of independence as presently understood by auditors participating in the study.

5 | RESEARCH PROBLEM AND METHODOLOGY

RESEARCH APPROACH

Two major considerations influenced the design and approach of this research.

■ There is considerable diversity in current EDP audit activities. While some audit staffs have been involved with EDP auditing for several years, a larger number are relatively new to the field.

■ It is important to know how internal auditors perceive the independence issue and how those who either rely on, or react to, EDP audit reports perceive the issue.

Because of the diversity of current EDP audit practice, a concerted effort was made to include in the sample companies with considerable EDP audit experience (especially design-phase audit experience) and companies with very little EDP audit experience. There was also interest in whether some of the key users of EDP audit reports weigh factors differently when evaluating the possible impairment of audit independence. Therefore, perceptions of internal audit independence were gathered from internal auditors, CPA's, heads of data processing operations, and members of top management.

A three-prong research approach utilizing hypothetical case situations, questionnaires, and interviews was used to gather reactions to factors that might influence internal audit independence. The case studies were used to study potential independence conflicts in a standardized environment. Thus, all the auditors participating in the study reacted to the same set of circumstances. The questionnaires and interviews gathered reactions to specific EDP audit activities and assessed the impact of various organizational and individual factors on internal audit independence.[11]

---

[11] See Appendix A for a sample of the questionnaires used in the study. For a more complete description of the research methodology, see Rittenberg, "The Impact of Internal Auditing During the EDP Application Design Process on Perceptions of Internal Audit Independence" in the Bibliography.

CHARACTERISTICS OF COMPANIES PARTICIPATING IN THE STUDY

The companies participating in the study were not randomly chosen but were selected according to predetermined criteria. Specifically, the sample included individuals with very little EDP audit experience and others with considerable EDP audit experience. The study also included both internal auditors and those who rely on, or react to, internal audit reports in the EDP area. These groups and the total number of participants are shown in Table 1.

Table 1
Study Participants by Major Groups

From the Internal Audit Function:		
Heads of internal auditing		21
EDP audit managers (heads of the EDP audit function)		39
EDP audit staff members		46
	Subtotal	106
Those Using the Internal Auditor's EDP Audit Work:		
Heads of data processing		28
Selected representatives of management (those to whom the head of internal auditing reports)*		25
Certified public accountants		39
	Subtotal	92
	Total	198

* Includes controllers, financial vice presidents, and, in several cases, company presidents.

All of the participants except the CPA's were from 41 of the nation's largest companies. Because it was preferred that the CPA's have experience with internal auditors performing EDP audit work, the CPA group was drawn from the external auditors of the companies included in the study.[12]

Approximately two-thirds of the participants (Table 2) were located in the Minneapolis-St. Paul area and Chicago. The remaining one-third was scattered throughout the United States. The 41 companies represented diverse lines of business.[13] Twenty-

[12] The CPA population was drawn primarily from six of the *Big 8* national CPA firms. Some key questions were also analyzed according to company affiliation. No significant pattern of responses emerged. The nonexistence of patterns plus some of the comments returned by the CPA's indicate that most of the issues addressed in the study are not codified in organization policy by the CPA firms.

[13] It is important to note that there was no difference in responses to the independence question that could be attributed to either the geographic locations or lines of business.

three companies had considerable EDP audit experience and a high degree of design-phase audit involvement, whereas 18 companies had minimal EDP audit experience and little or no design-phase involvement. A more detailed description of the sample companies is included in Appendix B.

Table 2
Geographic Dispersion of Sample Population

Location of Companies		Number	Percent
Minneapolis-St. Paul area		18	44%
Chicago		8	20%
Other U.S. cities		15	36%
	Total	41	100%

6 | RESEARCH RESULTS

RESULTS OF PARTICIPANTS' RESPONSES TO HYPOTHETICAL CASE STUDIES

Two hypothetical case studies were used in which internal auditors and CPA's assessed the likelihood of independent postinstallation audits where internal auditors previously performed design-phase audits. These cases presented a standardized environment to the participants; in other words, they rated other auditors in a controlled environment, rather than themselves in their own widely-diverse environments.[14]

Two cases were presented to the participants. The first case depicted the potential conflict of interests involved when auditors perform both design-phase and postinstallation audits of application controls (Figure 3, cell *A*). The other case depicted the potential conflict when auditors perform operational design-phase and postinstallation audits (Figure 3, cell *D*). The participants then rated a series of cases where, in addition to design-phase involvement, factors to be considered included assignment of different auditors to postinstallation audits, the auditor's technical EDP competence, and the reporting level of the head of internal auditing.

These factors and the alternatives applicable to them are summarized in Table 3 and will be discussed in more detail in the next two sections.

The Application Control Audit Case Studies

These cases depicted various conflicts that might arise when auditors perform design-phase and postinstallation audits of application controls. Internal auditors and CPA's were presented with a series of six cases[15] in which each of the factors took on one of the alternative values described in Table 4. All six cases included each of the factors and an associated value from those listed in

---

[14] The auditors also rated themselves in their own environment, as discussed later in this chapter.

[15] Twelve situations were possible; but to minimize the time commitment of the participants, each rated only half of the cases. However, all 12 situations were rated under a prearranged design.

Table 4.[16] The research design is known as a "3×2×2 factorial analysis of variance design." The purpose of the design is to enable us to determine what factors (variables) caused the greatest variance in the rating of the likelihood of an independent postinstallation audit.

Usable responses were obtained from 84 internal auditors and 30 CPA's. The following factors were significant (at the .01 level) and explained most of the variation in the participants' responses:

- Internal audit reporting level — Auditors reporting to the vice-presidential level were perceived as more independent than auditors reporting to the controller.
- Level of auditor participation during design phase and assignment of auditors to each phase.

Table 3
Factors and Alternative Values Studied in Case Studies

Factor	Value
Level of auditor participation during design phase	Four distinct alternatives were tested ranging from no participation to performing compliance tests to consulting activities.
Assignment of auditors to design phase and postinstallation phase of the audit	The same auditor could be assigned to each phase or different auditors could be assigned for postinstallation.
Auditor's technical EDP competence (background)	Auditors could have a primary background in either accounting or EDP. The EDP individual was presumed more knowledgeable in EDP, whereas the accountant was more knowledgeable in auditing.
Internal audit reporting level	The head of internal auditing could report to either the controller or the vice president of finance.

[16] It should be noted that, in this particular set of cases, variables *A* and *B* (design-phase participation and assignment of auditors) must be just one variable because, obviously, one could not assign different auditors to the postinstallation audit when none participated during the design phase. This variable could have three values: (1) no participation, (2) participation — same auditors for each phase, or (3) participation — different auditors for each phase.

Further analysis is required of the participants' reactions to design-phase auditing and the assignment of auditors to postinstallation audits. The mean ratings for independent post-installation audits for each of the three potential combinations of design-phase participation and auditor assignment are shown in Table 5. These ratings say that an independent postinstallation application control audit is more likely when an auditor *participates* during the design phase but a *different auditor* performs the postinstallation audit than when there is *no auditor participation* during the design phase. However, when the *same auditor* is assigned to both the design-phase and postinstallation phases, the likelihood of an independent postinstallation audit decreases dramatically.

Explaining the higher rating when different auditors are assigned to both phases, in comparison to no design-phase audit participation, many auditors interviewed felt the knowledge obtained during the design phase enables the Internal Audit Department to be less dependent on the EDP Department in determining and performing alternative approaches to post-installation audits. They saw design-phase audit participation as beneficial if the department had *sufficient personnel* to assign different auditors to the postinstallation audit.

Table 4
Variable Combinations Used in Application Control Case

Variable	Potential Values 1	Potential Values 2
A. Level of auditor participation during design phase	Does not participate	Application control review
B. Assignment of auditors to design and postinstallation phases	Same auditor for each phase	Different auditors
C. Auditor's technical EDP competence (background)	EDP trained	Auditor trained
D. Internal audit reporting level	Controller (at same level as head of data processing)	VP of finance (higher than controller)

Table 5
Ratings of Likelihood of Independent Postinstallation Audits Analyzed According to Auditor Design-Phase Participation and Assignment*

Auditor Design-Phase Participation	Mean Independence by Rating	
	Internal Auditors*	CPA's*
1. The auditor does not participate during the design phase.	3.56	3.50
2. The *same* auditor performs both design-phase and postinstallation audit activities.	3.15	3.27
3. *Different* auditors perform design-phase and postinstallation audit activities.	3.89	3.83
4. Mean response overall within group.	3.53	3.53

* The likelihood of an independent postinstallation audit was ranked on a 5-point scale. A rating of *3* was labeled "satisfactorily independent."

The Operational Audit Cases

The operational audit cases explored the potential loss of independence in a situation where internal auditors performed both design and postinstallation audits (Figure 3, cell *D*). This set of cases was presented only to internal auditors. All of the variables, except design-phase involvement, were the same as in the application control cases (Table 4).[17] Design-phase audit involvement was depicted as either of the following:

- Tests of compliance with prescribed EDP application development policies
- Auditor involvement encompassing compliance tests plus consulting or design-participation activities

Since there were four variables, each of which could take on either of two values, there were 16 possible combinations of variables and values. Again, to reduce the time commitment of the participants, each rated only eight of the situations. The following variables were found to explain most of the variation (at the .01 level of significance) in the ratings of independent postinstallation audits:

[17] See Appendix A for case background.

Level of design-phase audit participation: The lower level of design-phase participation (tests of compliance) was rated higher in independence than the higher level of participation (auditor involvement as a consultant or designer).

Assigning different auditors to the postinstallation audit: Assigning a different auditor to the postinstallation audit significantly increased the rating of likelihood of an independent postinstallation audit.

Internal audit reporting level: Reporting to a higher organizational level was rated much higher than reporting to a lower organizational level.

The interaction of the level of design-phase auditing with the assignment of different auditors: Discussion of this interaction follows.

In rating the interaction of design-phase involvement and auditor assignments, the participants considered the effect of both variables acting together. This can best be seen in Table 6 which indicates that when different auditors are assigned to both phases the type of design-phase participation does not affect the ratings of independent postinstallation audits. However, if the same auditor is assigned to both design and postinstallation audits, the participants felt the likelihood of an independent postinstallation audit dropped significantly, especially when the auditor acted as a consultant or participant during the design phase.

Table 6
Participants' Ratings Analyzed by Auditors' Design-Phase Audit Involvement and Assignment

Type of Design-Phase Audit Participation	Rating of Likelihood of Independent Postinstallation Audit When Auditors Are Assigned as Follows:	
	Same Auditor to Both Phases	Different Auditor for Postinstallation Audit
Compliance review	3.21*	3.76*
Consultant or participant	2.83*	3.77*

* The likelihood of an independent audit was rated on a 5-point scale and based on responses from 84 internal auditors. A rating of *3* was labeled "satisfactorily independent."

Table 7
Analysis of Operational Case Study Results by Level of Participants' EDP Audit Experience

Variables	Significance of Variable on Ratings of Likelihood of Independent Post-installation Audits	
	High Design-Phase Involvement Group	**Low Design-Phase Involvement Group**
Level of auditor participation during design phase	Not significant	Significant*
Assignment of different auditors to postinstallation audit	Significant*	Significant*
Internal audit reporting level	Significant*	Not significant
Interaction of level of design-phase involvement and assignment of auditors	Significant**	Not significant

* Computed at .01 level of statistical significance, using factorial analysis of variance model.
** Computed at .05 level of statistical significance, using factoring analysis of variance model.

A REANALYSIS OF RESULTS CONSIDERING THE PARTICIPANTS' EDP AUDIT EXPERIENCE

The previous analysis treated all internal auditors as a single group. However, the sample companies differed considerably in design-phase audit experience and overall EDP audit experience. Based upon a review of such factors as (a) the design-phase audit activities performed by the audit staffs, (b) the percentage of audit time spent in design-phase auditing, (c) the size of the EDP audit staff, and (d) the years of EDP audit experience, the sample was divided into two distinctively different groups:

- Low design-phase involvement group (18 companies)
- High design-phase involvement group (23 companies)

Because of the differences, the results of the operational case studies were analyzed separately for each group. The distinctions between them, summarized in Table 7, are striking. The highly involved, more experienced group was more influenced by the *interaction* of design-phase auditing and assignment of personnel to the postinstallation audits than by the type of design-phase audit performed. In other words, they said that the effect of design-phase auditing on independence depends on *both* the type of activities performed and whether separate auditors are assigned to the postinstallation audit. The less involved group, on the other hand, focused on the variables acting separately rather than on the interaction of variables. It is also interesting to note that the highly involved group attached greater importance to the auditors' reporting level than did the less involved group.[18]

The differences between the two groups suggest that perceptions of design-phase involvement and independence may be strongly influenced by the auditors' experiences with such activities. Those who have experienced the activities do not perceive a problem,[19] whereas those who have not are fearful of an independence conflict. Thus, views of independence may change as auditors and others become more familiar with design-phase auditing.

AUDIT INDEPENDENCE IN PARTICIPATING COMPANIES

The case studies required auditors to rate the independence of other auditors in hypothetical situations. In order to focus on the participants' current environment, everyone except the CPA's rated the independence of internal auditors in their organization when performing four different types of audits. These ratings are summarized in Table 8. All the ratings are above 3.00, a level labeled "satisfactorily independent." However, design-phase audits were rated significantly lower than the postinstallation audits.

The data in Table 8 were also reanalyzed according to the auditors' design-phase experience (see discussion under case studies). Upon reanalysis, a significant difference was found in the responses from the heads of EDP departments. The EDP department heads in companies with experienced design-phase auditors felt auditors were more independent when performing design-phase audits (mean = 4.3, a satisfactory level) than did the EDP department heads in companies with less experienced auditors (mean = 2.3, an unsatisfactory level). There appear to be two possible reasons for the higher independence ratings attached to design-phase auditing in companies with greater design-phase audit involvement.

---

[18] An interesting but speculative question arises at this time. Does the more experienced group's recognition of the importance of the auditors' organization status (reporting levels) partially explain why they are performing design-phase audit activities while the less involved group does not perform such activities?

[19] It should be noted that the group with high design-phase audit involvement has, for the most part, avoided activities that are perceived to have a negative effect on the auditor's independence.

Table 8
Ratings of Internal Audit Independence for Different Audit Activities

Type of Audit Activity	Mean*	Ratings of Independence on a 5-point Scale by:				
		EDP Audit Manager	Head of Internal Audit	EDP Audit Staff	Manage-ment	Head of EDP
1. Conducting a *control-oriented* audit of an installed EDP application	4.44	4.69	4.77	4.18	4.52	4.03†
2. Conducting an *information system postaudit* (the review and analysis of an implemented information system)	4.23	4.50	4.60	3.96	4.27	3.83
3. Conducting a management audit of an EDP center (the periodic or continuous evaluation of the organizational and operational efficiency of an EDP center)	4.09	4.48**	4.23	3.80	4.29	3.67
4. Participating in and reviewing activities during the *design phase* of an EDP application	3.84	4.19**	4.00	3.89	3.83	3.32
Number of responses	152	38	21	45	25	23

* Represents the simple mean of the five groups, assuming that the calculated group mean is representative of the mean for that group. Ratings were based on a 5-point scale with a *3* labeled "satisfactorily independent."

** Only 35 rated these activities because some of the auditors did not perform these audits.

† Twenty-six rated the control-oriented audit.

First, the companies with high design-phase involvement are careful to avoid audit activities where the auditor is viewed as a participant in the design. During the interviews, many of these auditors pointed out that part of the key to their success was convincing the EDP Department that the adequacy of the application was the responsibility of users and the EDP Department.

Second, perceptions of independence are based on either what the auditor has done or what someone expects the auditor to do. In companies with low design-phase involvement, the head of the EDP Department may expect something worse than what actually happens when internal auditors become more involved. This implies a learning effect associated with perceptions of independence. Furthermore, perceptions of independence may be influenced by the auditor's actions and by communication of the role auditing plays in EDP.

The findings shown in Table 8 indicate that perceptions of auditor independence are affected by the types of EDP audit activities conducted. Furthermore, perceptions of auditor independence may change as the observer becomes familiar with the design-phase audit activities.

INDEPENDENCE AND TYPE OF DESIGN-PHASE AUDIT ACTIVITIES PERFORMED

As noted earlier, there is considerable variation in the type of design-phase audit activities that might be conducted. An analysis of EDP design-phase audit activities currently performed led to the following categorization:

- Audit of the adequacy of application controls
- Performance of compliance tests of general controls
- Performance of expert-consultive activities relating to control aspects of new EDP developments
- Participation as a member in various design activities

A set of nine design-phase audit activities was formulated to represent these categories. Each participant was asked whether performance of the activity would likely impair the auditor's independence in a postinstallation audit and, if so, whether the Internal Audit Department could offset the loss of independence by assigning different auditors to the postinstallation audit. A summary of responses is presented in Table 9.

As seen in the table, the designer-participant activities were seen by a majority of the respondents as having a negative effect on the auditor's independence. On the other hand, compliance-testing activities had little effect on most respondents. The other activities had some negative impact which could be offset for virtually all respondents by assigning different auditors to the postinstallation audit.

Table 9
Summary of Effect of Specific Design-Phase Activities on Perceptions of Internal Audit Independence*

Design-Phase Audit Activity	Percent Perceiving Negative Impact on Independence (i.e., Decreased Independence)	Percent Believing Negative Impact Would Be Offset by Assigning Different Auditors to Post-audits	Percent Who Feel Negative Effect Will Not Be Offset by Assigning Different Auditors
Application Control Activities			
Specify audit trail and control requirements	34%	25%	9%
Recommend control to be installed	29%	24%	5%
Compliance Tests of General Controls			
Review design activities to assess adherence to company policies	9%	7%	2%
Expert-Consultant Activities			
Assess potential risks of proposed EDP application; report risks to management	19%	13%	6%
Report on reasonableness of time and cost estimates	22%	10%	12%
Review EDP application feasibility study for reasonableness and compatibility with present facilities; and report to management	27%	16%	11%

Designer Participant Activities			
Sign off at end of each major design phase, noting approval or specifying deficiencies	37%	25%	12%
Assist in design of needed processing controls	64%	42%	22%
Act as a liaison between programmers, users, and systems design personnel	70%	21%	49%
Mean Response	34.5%	20.3%	14.2%

* Based on responses from all groups, the total number responding to this was 181.

Table 10
Comparison of EDP Departments' and Managements' Ratings with Auditors' Ratings of Expert-Consultant Activities

	Percentage Indicating Performance of Activity Would Decrease Independence		
Expert-Consultant Design-Phase Activities	**Mean Response — Auditors****	**Mean Response — EDP and Management****	**Level of Significance of Difference***
Assess potential risks of proposed application	11.75	25.5	.01
Report on reasonableness of time and cost estimates	14.25	34.50	.001
Review feasibility study for reasonableness	17.25	42.5	.01

* Student's *t* distribution with 47 degrees of freedom.
** Average of responses from groups taken from Table 9.

The application control activities were rated somewhat more negatively than initially expected. Subsequent interviews with EDP audit managers indicated that the approach taken is the predominant influencing factor. Some participants felt that "specifying audit trails" or "recommending controls" might cause the auditors to be viewed as designers. In the interviews, auditors indicated that a preferred approach to specifying audit trails is to identify control problems and, only when necessary, to outline alternatives to solving the control problems. Moreover, EDP audit managers emphasized that responsibility for adequate controls lies with the EDP Department and the users involved with the project, not the auditors.

Some differences were noted among the groups of participants. On the whole, representatives of top management and heads of EDP departments perceived a more negative effect on independence as a result of the audit activities than did the audit groups. In particular, top management and EDP department heads were more negative toward the expert-consultant activities (see Table 10). It is possible that the activities cited under the expert-consultant heading (assessing potential risks, reporting on the reasonableness of time and cost studies, reviewing feasibility studies) may be viewed by EDP personnel and management as falling outside the auditors' scope. Thus, it would seem that internal auditors performing those activities should make a considerable effort to inform these groups of the nature of their audit work. Alternatively, the auditors should consider whether the activities fall within the auditors' scope envisioned in the *Statement of Responsibilities of Internal Auditors.*

In summary, auditors considering design-phase audit involvement should work on effectively communicating the nature of their audit activities to all affected parties. They should clearly communicate the nature of responsibility assumed (or lack of it) to the EDP Department and management.

IMPORTANCE OF ORGANIZATIONAL AND INDIVIDUAL FACTORS ON PERCEPTIONS OF INTERNAL AUDIT INDEPENDENCE

Internal audit independence may be affected by factors other than the auditor's design-phase audit involvement. Indeed, as we have seen, some factors, such as how auditors are assigned to design-phase and postinstallation audits, may be influential in offsetting negative effects that might be associated with design-phase audit involvement.

A review of the concept of internal audit independence led to the identification of 14 factors that are potentially influential on perceptions of internal audit independence. These factors were broadly classified into three categories: organizational factors, individual factors, and factors influenced or controlled by the Internal Audit Department.

Each participant in the study was asked to rate the importance of each factor to the independence of internal auditors conducting examinations in the EDP area. Included among the factors were the four variables assessed in the case studies. These variables were presented first since participants had already assessed their relative importance. The average rating (based on a ten-point scale) and relative ranking for each factor is presented in Table 11.

The results in Table 11 yield some interesting observations:

- Organizational factors, especially top management support, were rated the highest in importance by virtually every group in the study.

- Assignment of different auditors to postinstallation audits (very significant in the case studies) was rated relatively low.

- EDP technical competence was rated quite high by most participants.

- Supervision and review of work papers — a departmentally-controlled factor — was rated third highest in importance.

- The organizational factors are clearly the most important. The individual factors are all moderately important, whereas the departmentally-controlled factors vary widely in importance.

ANALYSIS OF FACTOR RATINGS

Organizational Factors

The importance of top management support for internal audit activities was reiterated by the participants. Moreover, the results indicate that the level of top management support is more important than the reporting level alone. The following comments are typical responses to these factors:

> *Top management support of all internal auditing is necessary if its independence and objectivity is to be developed, maintained, and recognized. Since EDP auditing is not traditional, is usually installed by necessity in a revolutionary rather than evolutionary manner, and should make challenges in a number of sensitive situations, it needs unqualified and oftentimes timely top management support* (from a member of management).

> *Top management's support, whether or not the auditor officially reports to it, has a very significant influence upon the ability of the auditor to function independently. If management has, and shows, genuine respect for the audit function and the importance of independence, the auditor's position is greatly enhanced* (from a CPA).

In summary, top management support fosters an independent audit environment wherein the auditor is encouraged to conduct

Table 11

Rating of Factors Affecting Internal Audit Independence in EDP Audit Environment

FACTORS AFFECTING INDEPENDENCE	Mean**	GROUPS* EDP Audit Managers	Heads of Internal Audit	Staff EDP Auditors	CPA's	Management
Organizational Factors						
Top management support	8.88^{1}	8.97^{1}	9.43^{1}	8.57^{1}	8.36^{1}	9.08^{1}
Level in organization to which head of internal audit reports	7.61^{2}	7.17^{2}	7.29^{5}	7.28^{2}	8.31^{2}	8.00^{3}
Individual Factors						
Personal characteristics of auditor	7.01^{4}	7.14^{3}	7.57^{3}	6.53^{5}	6.24^{7}	7.56^{4}
Auditor's technical EDP competence	6.91^{5}	6.45^{6}	6.52^{10}	6.57^{4}	6.87^{4}	8.12^{2}
Factors Influenced or Controlled by the Internal Audit Department						
Supervision and review of work papers	7.07^{3}	6.83^{4}	7.57^{4}	6.13^{9}	7.74^{3}	Not Rated
Adherence to professional code of ethics	6.79^{6}	6.38^{7}	7.71^{2}	6.45^{7}	5.92^{8}	7.48^{5}
Level of auditor's participation in design phase	6.71^{7}	6.72^{5}	6.95^{8}	6.64^{3}	6.25^{6}	7.00^{6}
Formality of audit reports	6.42^{8}	5.97^{10}	7.00^{6}	6.53^{6}	6.67^{5}	5.92^{10}
Responsibility assumed by signing off on design-phase activities	6.12^{9}	5.93^{11}	6.95^{7}	6.21^{8}	5.51^{10}	6.00^{9}
Assignment of different auditors to postinstallation audits	6.06^{10}	6.24^{8}	6.62^{9}	5.53^{11}	5.92^{8}	6.00^{8}
Staff turnover as department objective	5.81^{11}	6.03^{9}	5.95^{11}	5.30^{12}	5.13^{11}	6.64^{7}
Time restrictions imposed on audits	5.29^{12}	5.66^{13}	4.65^{14}	5.60^{10}	4.92^{12}	5.56^{11}
Evaluation methods for reviewing audit staff	5.14^{13}	4.69^{14}	5.62^{13}	5.21^{13}	4.77^{13}	5.40^{12}
Project composition, such as use of team approach on audits	5.08^{14}	5.76^{12}	5.91^{12}	5.19^{14}	4.28^{14}	4.26^{12}

Mean of All Items	6.49	6.42	6.84	6.27	6.21	6.69
Number of Responses	160	29	21	47	39	24

Note: Participants rated factors on the following scale:
1 - 3 Not important
4 - 7 Moderately important
8 - 10 Very important

* The superscript number represents the ranking of the item within that group.
** Represents the simple mean of the five groups.

audits and give opinions without adverse pressure from the departments audited. A high reporting level promotes internal audit independence by removing pressures from critiquing one's superior and providing an overall company perspective independent of any single department's influence.

Assignment of Auditors to Postinstallation Audits

The low rating attached to assigning different auditors to postinstallation audits contradicts the previous high rating in the case studies. Some participants felt that assigning different auditors is the only way to offset the negative impact of design-phase participation. Many participants felt other factors mitigated the possible loss of independence.

A number of the practicing internal auditors said they structure their design-phase involvement to minimize independence conflicts and that countervailing organizational factors tend to minimize independence conflicts. Conversations with experienced EDP auditors yielded the following reasons for attaching less importance to the assignment of different auditors to postinstallation audits:

Time constraints — Because of the demands on the auditor's time, there is usually a considerable time lag before the auditor can review the application again. Systems and applications change over time, so the auditor is forced to look at the application with a fresh approach.

Audit responsibility during design phase — Most auditors participating during the design phase focus on application control adequacies and prepare memos highlighting potential weaknesses. Subsequent investigations are considered follow-ups and are not viewed as conflicts of interest. When auditors sign off during the design phase, they clearly indicate it is for a particular time and that the systems are expected to change. Hence, the auditors do not feel "locked in" to any particular position.

Postinstallation audit coverage by regular internal audit staff — A trend in many large Internal Audit departments is a separate EDP audit section concentrating on design-phase audit work and assisting other internal auditors covering an EDP application as part of their normal audit. This relieves the need for assigning different auditors because the other auditors act as an independent check on the EDP audit section.

Importance of Technical EDP Competence and Personal Factors

Interviews with the participants regarding the issue of competence followed a similar theme: To be independent, the auditor must have adequate technical knowledge of EDP. The following comments summarize the attitude of most participants:

Auditors must have a working technical knowledge of EDP so they can review and evaluate systems on their own without relying on EDP personnel (from an internal auditor).

A high level of technical skills permits auditors to perform with little or no reliance on systems and data processing personnel (from a member of management).

EDP auditors must be technically competent because they will be dealing with technicians . . .To be effective, auditors must be able to communicate with technicians at the technicians' level and know when they are being "snowed" (from a CPA).

Technical EDP competence alleviates dependence on the EDP Department by developing self-reliance and the ability to reach independent judgments. Technical EDP competence is also necessary for quality audit work.

Most of the participants recognize that, in addition to competence, personal characteristics are important to individual action. For example:

If auditors are "independent thinkers," they can overcome many of the other obstacles to independence. They may even overcome the reporting system (from management).

Personal characteristics of auditors can override any of the other factors. Integrity, strength of character, good judgment, and keen perception of relationships, etc., are very significant factors which affect auditors' ability to be independent, especially in the EDP area. Otherwise, they must lean on those being examined (from a CPA).

Supervision and Review of Audit Work

Supervision and review of audit work was rated high by all groups except the staff auditors (ironically, the ones subject to the review). It was felt that this independent review within the Internal Audit Department promotes independent audits by providing an objective review and communicating the importance of independence. Comments from internal auditors included:

A review is necessary to make sure that personal feelings do not interfere with objectivity.

Good supervision can help remind auditors that they must be independent.

The CPA group is one of the strongest supporters of more supervision and review as exemplified in the following comments:

Knowledge that all their work will be subject to review should affect their independent attitude as well as the thoroughness of their work and documentation.

This provides an independent evaluation of audit findings and provides a check against undue influence by the department being audited.

Level of Design-Phase Audit Participation

Analysis of the ratings of design-phase audit participation reveals an interesting disparity. Many thought that participation during the design phase influences the auditor and thereby impairs objectivity. Others, emphasizing their view that design-phase involvement is only a review process, felt that properly conducted design-phase involvement facilitated independent postinstallation audits through increased knowledge and competence to audit the application and a higher probability that controls will be designed into the application that the auditor can use or test in the postinstallation audit.

The following responses are typical of the first (negative) view:

Involvement in design phase can only lead to overfamiliarity and accountability for initial results, both of which deter independence (from management).

If internal auditors participate greatly in setting up a new system, it becomes very difficult to later evaluate the system and find fault with it (from a CPA).

The other participants emphasized benefits of such participation if the auditor does not act as a designer:

If auditors participate fully during the design phase, but not performing control design, they can really learn what the system is all about (from an internal auditor).

Complete audit results cannot be obtained if the program design doesn't provide the proper audit trail or proper access to the program and the data (from a member of management).

Differences Among the Perceiver Groups

There is a great deal of consistency in the relative ranking of the factors in Table 11 by internal auditors and the other participants. The heads of internal audit and management attached to the factors the highest ratings of importance, whereas the staff auditors and CPA's rated most items lower. Some of the other differences include:

Management rated technical EDP competence higher than the other groups.

Heads of internal auditing placed greater emphasis on items partially influenced by the Internal Audit Department such as a professional code of ethics, supervision and review of work papers, and formal audit reports. They placed comparatively less emphasis on the technical EDP competence than did the other groups.

Certified public accountants placed less emphasis on individual factors and considerably more emphasis on other factors subject to formal review or testing. The factors rated relatively high by the

CPA's include supervision and review of work papers, formality of audit reports, top management support, and internal audit reporting level.

Staff EDP auditors rated supervision and review of work papers substantially lower and level of design-phase participation relatively higher than the other groups did.

The results presented in this section add another perspective to the narrower question of the effect of design-phase participation on perceptions of internal audit independence. Internal audit independence in an EDP environment is significantly influenced by factors other than the level of auditor participation during the design phase. Based on these results, it appears that auditors working in the EDP area and considering design-phase participation in new EDP application developments have two concerns in the following order:

- First, maximize independence by promoting the factors most important to internal audit independence as shown in Table 11.
- Then, when becoming involved with design-phase audits, avoid activities where the auditor might be viewed as a designer. Whenever possible, assigning different auditors to postinstallation audits should be considered. The need to assign different auditors will depend on the type of audit activities performed.

WHAT EDP AUDITORS CAN DO TO STRENGTHEN INDEPENDENCE

After assessing the results in the previous sections, it is interesting to know what participants felt EDP auditors *in their organizations can do now to strengthen independence.* Each participant was asked how their organizations' EDP auditors could strengthen independence while making the same contribution in the EDP area.[20] The group responses are presented in Table 12.

The overwhelming response (75%) favored auditors' increasing their technical EDP knowledge. The alternative of recruiting employees with more extensive EDP experience was rated significantly lower at 44%. This confirms other results which emphasize the importance of an "audit trait" often found in accountant-type auditors. The preference seems to be toward increasing the competence of the auditor rather than instilling an audit trait into a technical EDP person. However, it is speculative at this point to indicate which background, accounting or EDP, helps make the best EDP auditors.

A significant number (46%) thought independence would be strengthened by assigning different auditors to postinstallation audits. Most participants felt their organizations had adequate top management support. The lack of support for assuming less design-

[20] Since CPA's deal with many companies, they were asked to answer the question in reference to their experience with EDP auditors.

Table 12
Summary of Responses on How EDP Auditors Can Strengthen Independence

Method to Increase Independence	Mean**	EDP Audit Managers	Heads of Internal Audit	Staff EDP Auditors	Management	Heads of EDP Department	CPA's
1. Increase technical EDP knowledge	75%	72%	81%	74%	88%	52%	80%
2. Assign different auditors to design-phase and postinstallation audits	46%	51%	48%	33%	50%	44%	49%
3. Recruit employees with more extensive EDP experience	44%	31%	52%	52%	46%	44%	39%
4. Obtain greater top management support	37%	26%	38%	41%	13%	32%	70%
5. Set up audit section specializing in EDP auditing	32%	26%	43%	28%	25%	16%	54%
6. Recruit employees with more extensive education (such as MBA's)	13%	8%	29%	9%	17%	4%	13%
7. Assume less responsibility for results during design phase	8%	8%	14%	0%	4%	*	15%
Average Percentage of Items Checked	37%	32%	44%	34%	35%	32%	46%
Number of Responses	194	39	21	46	24	25	39

* Item not rated by this group.
** Simple mean of the six groups.

phase audit responsibility indicates that most auditors now performing design-phase audits are not perceived to be assuming too much responsibility. A significant portion of those companies without a separate EDP audit section (approximately 75%) said that setting up such a section would strengthen independence.

When viewing Table 12 responses by groups, it is noted that, in comparison with other groups, the CPA's placed greater emphasis on the factors of EDP competence, management support, and separation of duties. Additionally, none of the 46 audit staff members thought auditors needed to decrease their responsibilities during the design phase, whereas a minority of CPA's and heads of internal audit felt they should.

SUMMARY OF RESULTS

The issue of design-phase auditing and independence was addressed from a number of different research approaches. Perceptions of internal audit independence and factors affecting independence were gathered from internal auditors, CPA's, members of top management, and heads of EDP departments. There was a great deal of consistency among the methods and the groups. The following points summarize most of the results:

- Internal auditors function in an environment dictated by the organization of which they are a part. The most important factors affecting perceptions of internal audit independence are organizational freedom and support.

- Individual-based factors, such as personal characteristics, are slightly less important than the organizational factors.

- The auditor's technical EDP competence is a primary factor affecting the appearance of audit independence. It is also a factor that can be heavily influenced by departmental actions.

- Most internal auditors presently performing EDP audit work seem to be minimizing factors that could have dysfunctional independence consequences (e.g., time restrictions, evaluation methods, etc.) or they simply do not perceive them as important.

- Independence checks within the Internal Audit Department (such as supervision and review of audit work papers or coordination of work with the non-EDP internal auditors) promote positive perceptions of internal audit independence.

- Assignment of different auditors to postinstallation audits takes on differing levels of importance, depending on the level of design-phase activities performed. In most cases, while assigning different auditors to postinstallation audits will increase perceptions of independence, there are other cases where it does not offset the negative effect associated with the activity (such as designer-participant activities) or where the assignment of auditors is not necessary because the activity does not have a negative effect on perceptions of independence (such as compliance testing activities).

■ The apparent responsibility assumed by internal auditors during the design phase significantly affects perceptions of internal audit independence. Internal auditors should avoid activities in which they might be perceived as designers or as participants in the design.

■ Although there are some differences of opinion between the groups participating in the study, the differences are overshadowed by agreement on most items.

■ Those organizations in which design-phase auditing is currently performed are much less negative on the independence issue than are the less involved participants. This effect associated with EDP auditing indicates that perceptions of factors may change over time as individuals become more aware of the nature of design-phase auditing.

■ Design-phase auditing does not need to impair internal audit independence. Internal Audit departments have considerable flexibility in structuring themselves to contribute during the design phase without impairing independence.

7 INDEPENDENCE AND CURRENT EDP AUDIT ACTIVITIES

PERFORMANCE OF DESIGN-PHASE AUDIT ACTIVITIES

In the previous chapter, reference was made to the fact that internal auditors have generally avoided the design-phase activities most likely to impair independence. This chapter presents data about the present conduct of design-phase auditing and discusses some trends in EDP auditing.

A summary of design-phase audit activities conducted by participants in this study is presented in Table 13. As seen in the table, the activities most performed are those least likely to impair audit independence such as reviewing for the adequacy of application controls and performing compliance tests of general controls. Assessing potential risks of proposed EDP applications is performed frequently. However, the auditors performing this activity indicated that they concentrate on security and audit risks rather than the risk that a proposed application would not achieve forecasted results. For the most part, auditors avoid audit activities in which they might be viewed as participants in the design process (items 10 through 13 of Table 13).

A substantial number of auditors (18 of 39) have either formal or informal sign-off responsibilities during major development phases. There may be, however, a trend away from formal reports during the design phase and toward the issuance of memos on an "as-needed basis." The types of reports issued during the design phase by the sampled companies are summarized in Table 14. The majority of these reports goes to the data processing and user groups for resolution at an early stage in the development process. When formal reports are issued, many auditors emphasize that their opinion covers a single point in the development and, thus, does not vouch for the adequacy of controls in the developed application.

Many EDP auditors in the sampled companies have some representation on or involvement with data processing committees. Responding to an exploratory question, all the auditors presently involved with EDP committees said such involvement does not

Table 13
Study Participants' Performance of Design-Phase EDP Audit Activities

Design-Phase EDP Audit Activity	Performance (Mean Response*)
1. *Identify audit trail* and control *requirements* for new EDP application; prepare alternative recommendations.	3.67
2. *Review design documentation* to assess *compliance* to company policies.	3.26
3. *Assess potential risks* of proposed EDP application; report risks to management.	3.21
4. Prepare audit guide for future audits of application.	3.00
5. Review design activities to assess *adherence* to company policy.	2.95
6. *Sign off* at end of each major design phase, noting approval or specifying deficiencies.	2.77
7. *Assist in* the *design* of needed processing controls for new EDP application.	2.74
8. *Review conversion tests* performed by others, identifying areas for further tests.	2.59
9. *Review* EDP application *feasibility study* for reasonableness and compatibility with present facilities and report to management.	2.54
10. *Participate* as part of team performing *conversion tests* before application goes "on stream."	2.23
11. Act as *liaison* between programmers, users, and system design personnel.	2.13
12. *Design* or supervise development of *embedded audit routines* to be included in EDP application program.	2.11
13. Participate as *member of feasibility* study committee, assessing appropriateness of proposed EDP application.	1.59

* Based on 39 responses from EDP audit managers. Performance of the activity was rated on a 5-point scale:

1 Never—Activity is not performed
2 Occasionally—Performed on less than 35% of major EDP application audits
3 One-half time—Performed on 35-65% of major EDP application audits
4 Usually—Performed on 65-95% of major EDP application audits
5 Always—Performed on 95-100% of major EDP application audits

Table 14
Type of Reports Issued by EDP Auditors During Design Phase

Type of Report Issued	Contents & Distribution	Number of Companies Issuing Reports*
Memos when required	Control & audit areas needing resolution. Copies go to data processing and major user groups.	17
Formal reports	Usually issued at end of major milestone. Comments include unresolved areas, control requirements, and opinion of project (at that time). Reports usually go to data processing and major user groups.	11
Early design phase (before programming)	Comments about needed control and audit requirements not yet included in data processing plans. Other specific comments are generally intended for users. Copies go to users and data processing.	6
Do not issue reports during design phase		13

* Some companies are included in more than one of the categories.
Source: Based on 39 responses from EDP audit managers.

impair independence. Although this response was initially surprising, an analysis of current auditor involvement with EDP committees presented in Table 15 indicates that auditors structure their EDP relationship carefully in order to avoid voting or design responsibilities.

The auditors' main function on most EDP committees is to provide input on the need for controls. Many auditors judged their EDP standards committee role as very important, enabling them to concentrate on testing adherence to established EDP standards. As noted earlier, tests of adherence to established policies or standards are not perceived to impair independence. Further interviews with selected EDP audit managers indicate that participation on some committees effectively serves to open up two-way communication which keeps the EDP auditor in touch with all major EDP developments.

Table 15
Types of EDP Auditor Involvement with Data Processing Committees

Data Processing Committee	EDP Auditor's Function on Committee	Number of Companies with Auditor Involvement with Committee
Committee formed for specific application	Meet with design team and user representatives. Point out control, audit, and security needs.	9
Data security	Create awareness of security and control needs and make recommendations.	5
EDP documentation of standards	Input on desirable standards. Also serves as a base for the auditor to compare actual procedures.	5
EDP steering	Non-voting member. Maintain awareness of upcoming projects. Provide expertise on security and controls.	3
Other	Postimplementation review teams. Review major program changes, other functions.	5
Not on committees	Although not on official committees, most of these departments have open lines of communication with data processing and receive copies of memos relating to new EDP developments and security provisions.	15

Source: Responses from 39 EDP audit managers.

OBJECTIVES OF EDP AUDITING

Internal auditing is defined as "an independent appraisal activity within an organization for the review of operations as a service to management.[21] Thus, it is interesting to know what EDP audit activities are of most concern to management. In that vein, members of top management and EDP internal auditors were asked to rate the importance of various EDP audit objectives. Their ratings of EDP audit objectives are summarized in Table 16.

The three highest-rated EDP audit objectives in Table 16 emphasize design-phase and postinstallation audit activities almost equally. In addition, the table shows that current audit objectives are more oriented to application controls (items *A, B, C, and H*) than to general controls or operational audits. It is also interesting that objectives calling for independent opinions on other than controls (such as item *G* — evaluate efficiency of EDP) were rated very low by management. Also, management placed more emphasis on coordinating work with the CPA than the internal auditor did.

CPA's WILLINGNESS TO RELY ON INTERNAL AUDIT OF EDP

Because the views of CPA's are important to management, it is well to note in Table 17 that CPA's participating in this study are willing to adjust the scope of their EDP audit activities when they are satisfied with the internal auditor's independence and quality of work. In addition, the CPA's strongly agreed that the internal auditor should evaluate the adequacy of controls during the design phase of new EDP application developments. The audit activities most likely to affect the scope of the CPA's audit include both design-phase and postinstallation audits.[22]

---

[21] *Statement of Responsibilities of Internal Auditors.*

[22] For a more complete discussion, see Larry E. Rittenberg and Gordon B. Davis, "Auditing Complex EDP Systems: The Relationship Between Internal and External Auditors," University of Wisconsin, School of Business, Working Paper, 1976.

Table 16
Rating of EDP Audit Objectives by Members of Top Management and EDP Auditors

EDP Audit Objective	Importance of Objective Rated by		Design-Phase or Postinstallation Audit Activity
	EDP Auditors*	Management*	
A. Review new EDP application during design phase to assess adequacy of controls.	1 (3.51)	3 (3.52)	Design phase
B. Test controls of installed system.	2 (3.49)	1 (3.71)	Postinstallation
C. Detect and/or deter fraudulent activity.	3 (3.14)	2 (3.60)	Both
D. Improve EDP development activities by making constructive recommendations.	4 (3.00)	7 (2.80)	Design phase
E. Review design activities for compliance with stated policies and procedures.	5 (2.90)	5 (3.04)	Design phase
F. Conduct postaudit of new EDP development to ascertain if projected results are achieved.	6 (2.69)	6 (2.92)	Postinstallation
G. Evaluate efficiency or effectiveness of EDP.	7 (2.64)	8 (2.44)	Postinstallation
H. Coordinate work with CPA to reduce or minimize external audit fee.	8 (2.21)	4 (3.25)	Generally postinstallation

* The first number represents the relative ranking of each objective within the group. The number in parentheses represents the rating of the objective on a 4.0 scale. Based on 39 responses from EDP audit managers and 25 responses from members of top management.

Table 17
CPA's Views on EDP Auditing

Statements	CPA's Agreement with Statement*
1. Other things being equal, CPA's should be able to adjust the scope of audit activities in the EDP area if they are satisfied with the "independence" of the internal auditor and have reviewed and tested samples of the internal auditor's work in the EDP area.	4.82
2. The internal auditor or EDP auditor should actively evaluate the adequacy of controls, security provisions, and so forth, during the design phase of a new major EDP application development.	4.59

* This is based on 39 responses from CPA's. Agreement was rated on the following scale:

5 Very strongly agree
4 Agree
3 Neither agree nor disagree
2 Disagree
1 Very strongly disagree

8 SUMMARY AND IMPLICATIONS

The major conclusion of this study is that performance of design-phase audit activities by internal auditors need not impair internal audit independence and that the advantages of design-phase audit participation may be substantial. Auditors, however, should carefully consider both the structure of the Internal Audit Department and the audit activities performed to determine the potential impact on audit independence.

The relationship of design-phase auditing and independence is illustrated in Figure 7. A number of factors, including the Internal Audit Department's philosophy, the system being developed, and management requests, will influence the auditors' involvement in developing a system. Audit involvement, the auditors' technical EDP competence, policies for assigning different auditors to post-installation audits, and so forth, will have a bearing on audit independence.

There are two aspects of audit independence: *real* and *perceived.* The auditors' real independence will affect periodic reviews and evaluation of system accomplishments which should lead to future design improvements and greater integrity of the ongoing system. The auditors' independence as perceived by others (data processing, users, management, CPA's) may impact on whether future systems design improvements are made and whether support and resources are furnished to foster effective audits. These bottom-line factors, together with design-phase audit involvement, contribute to the key element of the entire process: the probability of successful and auditable systems development.

RECOMMENDATIONS FROM STUDY

The study concludes that the independence issue should not deter auditors from performing design-phase audits. However, the auditors should consider carefully the audit activities to be performed. The following recommendations are intended to promote effective design-phase audit involvement without jeopardizing internal audit independence.

Figure 7
A Model of EDP Auditing and Internal Audit Independence

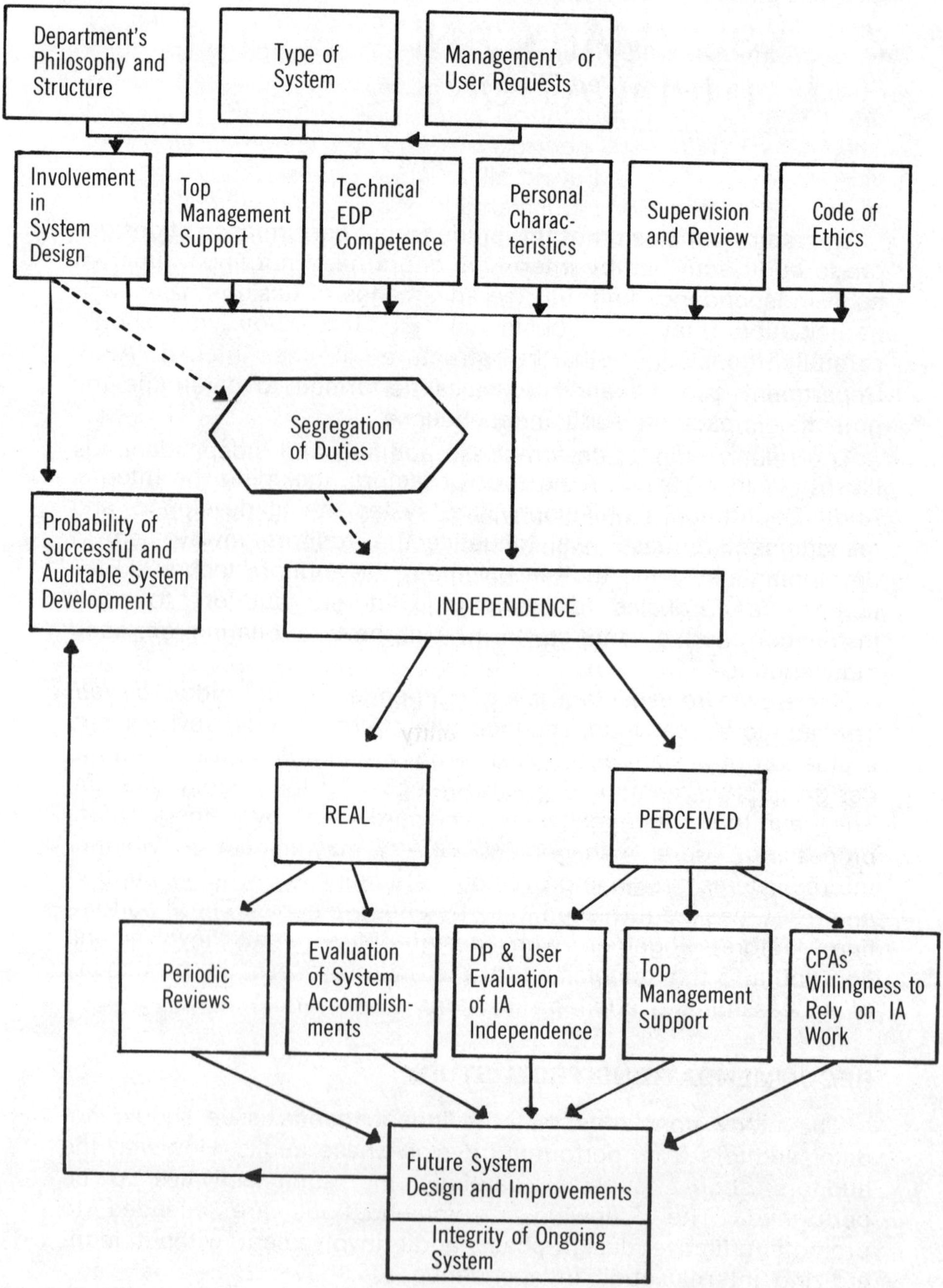

Performance of Design-Phase Audit Activities

The arguments for design-phase audit participation (for example, complexity of new systems and the need to insure auditability) are persuasive. Since the independence issue should not be a major deterrent, it is *recommended that internal auditors become involved during the design phase of new EDP applications,* provided, of course, that the auditor is competent. *The design-phase audit activities should be limited to reviewing, testing, and assessing the adequacy of application controls and reviewing the adequacy and compliance with general controls over the application development process.* Auditors should avoid all activities in which they might be viewed as designers or participants in designing new applications.

The control being reviewed (application versus general) does not affect perceptions of independence. Therefore, operation-oriented, design-phase audits need not be incompatible with internal audit independence.

If auditors become involved during the design phase at low levels such as reviewing for adequacy of controls or testing compliance with procedures, it is not necessary to assign different auditors to postinstallation audits. Nevertheless, assigning different auditors to postinstallation audits has a positive effect on perceived independence for all except the designer-participant activities.

Auditors should not become full-time voting participants on a committee charged with the design of a new EDP application. Auditors may make themselves available to the committee as reviewers or consultants, however. It is important that auditors acting as consultants recognize their duty to point out control weaknesses. They may, perhaps, outline alternative solutions, but they should not assume responsibility for the adequacy of the controls installed.

It is imperative that data processing personnel be control conscious. Nonauditors have a tendency to rely on auditors as control experts who should be involved in designing controls. It is difficult in some organizations to convince data processing and user departments that they have the primary responsibility for the design, adequacy, and testing of controls. Often the most effective way to establish this understanding is to include control standards and testing procedures in the formal data processing standards. Such inclusion has the following advantages for auditors in aiding them to retain their independence:

- Responsibility for controls is clearly defined.
- Because the standards are defined, EDP personnel are likely to take more initiative in designing and testing controls.
- The standards provide a basis against which a particular application development can be evaluated. The auditor can make an

overall assessment of the adequacy of the standards. Once that is done, it does not need to be repeated. The auditor's task then becomes one of evaluating adherence to the standards — an activity which is not perceived to lead to a loss of independence.

Auditors must be continually conscious of the pressures to become active designers or consultants in the design of new systems. Such pressures should be resisted although, as stated earlier, auditors should be willing to point out areas of control weaknesses and, perhaps, alternative approaches.

Promoting Technical EDP Competence

Auditors' EDP competence is perceived to affect their self-reliance and thus their independence. Therefore, internal auditors *must devote the necessary resources to build competence in any design-phase audit area subject to review.* It is suggested that EDP audit training be included in the Internal Audit Department's budget. In addition to the many courses offered by The Institute of Internal Auditors, the Internal Audit Department should also consider sending auditors to other seminars that data processing personnel attend.

Recognizing and Cultivating Organizational Relationships Conducive to Independence

Top management support was rated the most important factor affecting perceptions of internal audit independence by all of the groups in the study. Closely related, and rated second in importance, was the reporting level (organization status) of the Internal Audit Department. Management support is recognized as a major source of internal auditors' authority and affects internal audit independence in three ways:

■ It facilitates freedom of access and program determination.

■ It relieves the auditor from pressures which might cause compromises in audit scope or audit opinions.

■ It improves the allocation of resources to the Internal Audit Department. This, in turn, allows the department to employ and train individuals with the required EDP competence and to utilize other departmentally controlled factors that promote independence: supervision and review, assignment of different auditors to postinstallation audits, and minimizing time constraints.

A high reporting level complements top management support and promotes internal audit independence by promoting a total company perspective.

In addition, there is a need to communicate to EDP management the scope and nature of internal audit activities. An EDP

Department's negative response to activities such as recommending controls and reviewing design-phase activities for adherence to company policies indicates unfamiliarity with internal auditing. *The internal auditor must devote more effort to communicating the role of internal audit in the organization* until it is clearly understood by all those affected.

Structuring the Internal Audit Department to Promote Independence

The Internal Audit Department must recognize the factors under its control and use them to maximum advantage. These factors include supervision and review of work, assigning auditors to tasks, auditor sign-off, The Institute of Internal Auditors' Code of Ethics, *and others.* The need for independence must be reiterated, especially when many new auditors might have a data processing background.

Supervision and review of work papers were rated very high as factors affecting independence. Supervision and review create an environment that promotes independence by communicating the importance of independent audits to the staff auditors, and providing an independent check on the audit.

Assigning different auditors is another factor to be considered. The need for different auditors may depend on the types of design-phase activities conducted, time lag between audits, and supervision and review of work papers by audit management.

Establishing Separate EDP Audit Sections

It is recommended that large organizations establish, where practicable, a separate EDP audit section of the Internal Audit Department. These EDP audit sections should perform design-phase audit activities and, when possible, coordinate postinstallation audits with other members of the internal audit staff. Establishing a separate audit section appears to offer the following advantages:

- The existence of the EDP audit section recognizes a commitment of the organization to EDP auditing. This commitment provides the assurance needed to develop an adequate training program or plan to increase the level of EDP audit competence.

- Coordinating postinstallation audits with other internal auditors offers two advantages: It can insure a "fresh look" at the application, and it can provide a broader coverage of postinstallation audits.

Smaller organizations should have at least one EDP audit specialist. The remaining staff auditors should develop the ability to conduct postinstallation audits.

CONCLUSION

The results of this study indicate that internal auditors can make important design-phase audit contributions to an organization without impairing independence. However, internal auditors must be constantly aware of potential threats to independence and must act continuously to maintain or increase independence. In considering EDP design-phase audit involvement, they should review the independence-related factors identified in this study. A carefully conceived plan of action will enable auditors to make a significant contribution to the organization without impairing the essential ingredient of internal auditing — independence.

SELECTED BIBLIOGRAPHY

Books

American Institute of Certified Public Accountants. *Restatement of the Code of Professional Ethics.* New York: American Institute of Certified Public Accountants, 1972.

American Institute of Certified Public Accountants. *Statement on Auditing Standards.* New York: American Institute of Certified Public Accountants, 1973.

American Institute of Certified Public Accountants. *Statement on Auditing Standards No. 3 — The Effects of EDP on the Auditor's Study and Evaluation of Internal Control.* New York: American Institute of Certified Public Accountants, 1974.

Barrett, Michael J. "Some Behavioral Attributes of Professional Audit Independence." PhD dissertation, University of Colorado, 1969.

Canadian Institute of Chartered Accountants. *Computer Control Guidelines.* Toronto: Canadian Institute of Chartered Accountants, 1970.

Canadian Institute of Chartered Accountants. *Computer Audit Guidelines.* Toronto: Canadian Institute of Chartered Accountants, 1975.

Carey, John L., and Doherty, William O. *Ethical Standards of the Accounting Profession.* New York: American Institute of Certified Public Accountants, 1966.

Comptroller General of the United States. *Standards for Audit of Governmental Organizations, Programs, Activities, and Functions.* Washington, D.C.: Government Printing Office, 1972.

Davis, Gordon B. *Computer Data Processing.* Second Ed. New York: McGraw-Hill Book Company, 1973.

Jancura, Elise J. *Audit and Control of Computer Systems.* New York: Petrocelli/Charter, 1974.

Keithley, Johnnie P. "The Importance of Auditing Standards in the Development of Internal Auditing as a Professional Field." PhD dissertation, University of Missouri, 1972.

Mair, William; Wood, Donald; and Davis, Keagle. *Computer Control and Audit.* Altamonte Springs, Fl: The Institute of Internal Auditors, 1976.

Mautz, Robert K., and Sharaf, Hussein F. *The Philosophy of Auditing.* New York: American Accounting Association, 1961.

Rittenberg, Larry E. "The Impact of Internal Auditing During the EDP Application Design Process on Perceptions of Internal Audit Independence." PhD dissertation, University of Minnesota, 1975.

Sawyer, Lawrence B. *The Practice of Modern Internal Auditing.* Altamonte Springs, Fl: The Institute of Internal Auditors, 1973.

Shaw, J. C., and Atkins, W. *Managing Computer System Projects.* New York: McGraw-Hill Book Company, 1970.

Articles

"Advanced EDP Systems and the Auditor's Concerns." *The Journal of Accountancy* (January 1975) : 66-72.

Alexander, Tom. "Waiting for the Great Computer Rip-Off." *Fortune* (July 1974) : 143-150.

Anderson, Rodney. "Computer Control: An Essential Commodity in Computer Systems Development." *The Internal Auditor* (April 1976) : 34-51.

Berryman, R. G. "Auditor Independence: Its Historical Development and Some Proposals for Research." *Contemporary Auditing Problems*. Howard F. Stettler, Editor. Lawrence, Kansas: University of Kansas Printing Service, 1974 : 1-15.

Canning, Richard G. "Computer Fraud and Embezzlement." *EDP Analyzer* (September 1973).

Canning, Richard G. "Protecting Valuable Data — Part II." *EDP Analyzer* (January 1974).

Canning, Richard G. "The Internal Auditor and the Computer." *EDP Analyzer* (March 1975).

Carolus, Roger N. "Some Challenges of Operational Auditing." *The Internal Auditor* (November-December 1969) : 12-27.

Cutting, Richard W., Guiltman, Richard J., Lilly, Fred L., Jr., and Mullarkey, John F. "Technical Proficiency for Auditing Computer Processed Records." *The Journal of Accountancy* (October 1971) : 74-77.

Dickson, Gary, and Powers, Richard F. "MIS Project Management: Myths, Opinions, Reality." Management Information Systems Research Center Working Paper Series, MISRC-WP-01, Minneapolis : University of Minnesota.

Emens, Kenneth L., and Milher, Allen G. "Auditing the Application System Proposal." *The Internal Auditor* (September-October 1974) : 57-60.

Glass, Donald. "Results-Oriented Auditing and Independence." *The Internal Auditor* (May-June 1975) : 25-28.

Hanson, Ernest. "Communicator Creditability and the Auditor." *New York Certified Public Accountant* (September 1969) : 679-684.

Harris, Richard D. "EDP System Audits." *Data Management* (September 1971) : 64-67.

Hartley, Ronald V., and Ross, Timothy L. "MAS and Audit Independence: An Image Problem." *The Journal of Accountancy* (November 1972) : 42-51.

Heeschen, P. E. "Auditing D. P. Administrative Activities: Operational Auditing Applied to EDP." *The Internal Auditor* (November-December 1970) : 55-62.

Holmes, Fenwicke. "Auditing from the DP Manager's Viewpoint." *The Internal Auditor* (November-December 1975) : 29-34.

Jancura, Elise. "Technical Proficiency Standards for Auditing Computer Processed Records." *The Journal of Accountancy* (August 1975) : 39-44.

Juranas, Louis. "Auditing in the Systems Design Environment." *The Internal Auditor* (September-October 1971) : 54-59.

Kelley, Donald. "Data Control: A Vital Link of Information Processing." *The Internal Auditor* (July-August 1975) : 39-44.

Keyes, Edward G. "The Auditor's Role in New Systems Development." *The Internal Auditor* (January-February 1973) : 31-38.

Levine, E. G. "Auditing Requirements for Advanced Systems." *The Journal of Accountancy* (March 1974) : 74-76.

Mason, John O. "Management Information Systems: The Auditors Role." *The Internal Auditor* (September-October 1975) : 40-48.

Matson, Morris C. "Systems Design and Internal Audit — An Effective Interface." *The Internal Auditor* (March-April 1972) : 48-53.

McFarlan, F. Warren. "Management Audit of the EDP Department." *Harvard Business Review* (May-June 1973) : 131-142.

Miller, Timothy. "EDP — A Matter of Definition." *The Internal Auditor* (July-August 1975) : 31-38.

Murray, T. J. "The Equity Funding Syndrome: A New Corporate Phobia." *Dun's Review* (September 1973) : 69-71.

Otto, James. "Operational Auditing Applied to Data Processing Facilities." *The Internal Auditor* (September-October 1971) : 31-43.

Pauley, Charles A. "Audit Responsibilities in the Design of Computerized Systems." *The Internal Auditor* (July-August 1969) : 23-32.

Perry, William E. "The Making of a Computer Auditor." *The Internal Auditor* (November-December 1974) : 11-22.

Rittenberg, Larry E., and Davis, Gordon. "Auditing Complex EDP Systems: The Relationship Between Internal and External Auditors." University of Wisconsin Working Paper, 1976.

Scanlan, Michael. "A Proposal for Alternative Procedures for Audit of Real-Time Data Systems." *The Internal Auditor* (November-December 1975) : 77-86.

Schaffer, Eleanor. "Auditing for the Future: Audit Review of Systems Development." *The Internal Auditor* (March-April 1975) : 61-67.

Sollenberger, Harold M., and Arens, Alvin A. "Systems Control and Post-Completion Systems Audit." *The Internal Auditor* (March-April 1973) : 22-23.

Taylor, Alan. "Let's Give the Internal Auditor Full Responsibility." *Computerworld* (November 22, 1973) : 8.

The Institute of Internal Auditors. "Should the Internal Auditor Help Develop EDP Programs." *The Internal Auditor* (January-February 1975) : 51-59.

The Institute of Internal Auditors. *Statement of Responsibilities of Internal Auditors.* Altamonte Springs, Florida: The Institute of Internal Auditors, 1971.

Wasserman, Joseph. "Control in an EDP Environment." *The Internal Auditor* (September-October 1970) : 40-50.

Weiss, Harold. "Computer Security: An Overview." *Datamation* (January 1974) : 42-47.

Weiss, Harold. "EDP Audit Job Descriptions." *EDPACS* (March 1974) : 7-11.

Wyatt, Arthur. "Competence and Independence in Auditing." *The Journal of Accountancy* (April 1972) : 71-74.

APPENDIX A

Sample of Questionnaires Used in the Study

Note: This questionnaire was sent to the head of internal auditing and EDP audit staff members. It is one of five questionnaires used in the study, included here because various parts were used in the questionnaires completed by the other participating groups.

INTERNAL AUDIT INDEPENDENCE QUESTIONNAIRE

Introduction:

The attached questionnaire is designed to gather your view of factors that might affect internal audit independence when auditors are involved during the design stages of new computer developments and subsequently perform audits of the installed system. The questionnaire is divided into two parts which can be completed independently from the other. Part I contains a series of statements and questions regarding your view of the audit environment in your firm and your perception of internal audit independence in your organization. Part II consists of a series of case situations designed to assess the importance of factors that might affect the ability of an internal audit department to conduct independent examinations of EDP applications when auditors have been involved during the development stages of an EDP application. If you have any questions regarding the research please contact me.

Larry E. Rittenberg
Ph.D. Candidate in Accounting
Graduate School of Business
University of Minnesota
Minneapolis, Minnesota 55455

Phone: 612-373-5849
612-636-7942

Company______________________________

Name______________________________

Department______________________________

Title______________________________

Number of years experience in EDP related auditing________________

Part I.

1. This section consists of a series of statements about departments such as yours. The purpose of this section is to find out how accurately these statements describe the audit environment in your organization. Please indicate how well each statement describes the internal audit atmosphere in your organization by marking one of the following categories: Very Well (VW), Well (W), Uncertain (?), Poorly (P), or Very Poorly (VP).

	Statement					
(1)	In this organization it is very difficult to admit a mistake.	VP	P	?	W	VW
(2)	An attempt is made to clear up negative findings rather than include them in a formal report.	VP	P	?	W	VW
(3)	Acceptance by, and good working relationships with the unit being audited is very important.	VP	P	?	W	VW
(4)	Since internal auditing is not considered a career position, it is important to establish good contacts with other departments.	VP	P	?	W	VW
(5)	Many jobs are scheduled under such tight time restrictions that it is not possible to do a thorough audit.	VP	P	?	W	VW
(6)	There is pressure to avoid making any department or individual look bad.	VP	P	?	W	VW
(7)	There is a strong feeling that the auditor should be very cognizant of, and adhere to the internal audit profession's Code of Ethics.	VP	P	?	W	VW
(8)	There are some jobs that contain so many restrictions that it is difficult to reach substantive conclusions.	VP	P	?	W	VW
(9)	It is important that the majority of recommendations made will be implemented by the department audited.	VP	P	?	W	VW
(10)	The internal audit position is sufficiently secure from outside pressures that an auditor can freely communicate his findings.	VP	P	?	W	VW

(11) There are certain areas of the organization where the auditor must be careful not to step on anyone's toes. | VP | P | ? | W | VW |

(12) The internal audit department is strongly supported by top management thus assuring freedom to determine audit scope and proper consideration of audit findings. | VP | P | ? | W | VW |

(13) In general, there are few restrictions on job selection, audit procedures, or report contents. | VP | P | ? | W | VW |

(14) In a sense, the auditor assumes some responsibility for the results of recommendations he makes. | VP | P | ? | W | VW |

(15) There are many audit situations, such as reviewing for the implementation of recommendations where it is difficult to remain truly objective. | VP | P | ? | W | VW |

2. Auditor independence may be defined as:

> "The ability of an auditor to conduct and fully report on the results of an audit without personal biases or prejudices; and to determine audit scope and audit techniques without adverse or controlling influence from the auditee or other managerial segments of the organization."

Using the above definition of independence, how would you rate the degree of auditor independence in this organization when you are performing the following activities?

a. Conducting a control oriented audit of an installed EDP application.

Not Independent		Satisfactorily Independent		Highly Independent
1	2	3	4	5

b. Conducting a management audit of an EDP center (The periodic or continuous evaluation of the organizational and operational efficiency of an EDP center).

Not Independent		Satisfactorily Independent		Highly Independent
1	2	3	4	5

c. Participating in, and reviewing activities during design phase of an EDP application.

Not Independent		Satisfactorily Independent		Highly Independent
1	2	3	4	5

d. Conducting an information system post audit (review and analysis of implemented information system).

Not Independent		Satisfactorily Independent		Highly Independent
1	2	3	4	5

3. How could the audit department in this organization strengthen its independence while making the same contribution in the EDP area? Check all that are applicable.

_____ Assign different auditors to design stage audit work and post-installation audit work.

_____ Increase EDP technical knowledge of audit personnel.

_____ Obtain greater top management support.

_____ Recruit employees with more extensive education (e.g., more M.B.A.'s).

_____ Recruit employees with more extensive EDP background and experience.

_____ Set up EDP audit section specializing in EDP auditing.

_____ Assume less responsibility for results during design phase.

_____ Other____

_____ Other____

_____ Other____

Part II. CASE SITUATIONS

Introduction:

Since each person responding to this questionnaire may be involved differently with EDP audits, a series of short standardized cases have been designed to elicit your responses to various situations where internal auditors are involved during the design stages of new computer developments. In each case you are asked to rate the likelihood that an independent audit of the type described can take place. For your rating of the case situations the following definition of independence is given:

> Independence: The ability of an auditor to conduct and fully report the results of an audit without personal biases or prejudices; and with the ability to determine audit scope and audit procedures without adverse or controlling influence from the auditee or other managerial segments of the organization. The objective of independence is to assure a fair, complete, and objective appraisal of the situation audited.

For your future reference the major activities of the design phases and operations phase of a computer application may be viewed as follows:

Design Phase	Operations Phase
1. Feasibility study	1. Operation and Maintenance
2. Systems Analysis and Design	2. Minor Program or Processing Changes
3. Procedure and Program Development	3. Periodic Assessment of Application Contribution
4. Testing and Conversion	

CASE SITUATIONS: NORMAL AUDIT OF EDP APPLICATION CONTROLS

The Control Audit:

In the case situations to follow, we are concerned with the ability of an internal audit department to conduct a normal, control oriented audit of a computer application during the operations phase. The objective of such an audit is the testing and evaluation of existing EDP controls. An example of this type of audit would be an evaluation and testing of controls applicable to a sales and accounts receivable EDP application.

The audit approach generally follows the following lines:

1. A review of controls via inquiry and questionnaire
2. A test for existence of controls
3. A test of controls during normal operation

Testing can be done by a variety of methods including tracing transactions, insertion of test data, or use of audit software to extract and verify data. Surprise visits may be made to view actual operations and procedures of the EDP center.

Factors to be Assessed:

The following four factors are considered in the cases:

1. Participation during System Design Phase

   There are two alternatives: No Participation, or Participation. If the auditor participates his role may be described as follows:

   "The auditor is concerned that controls are designed into the system during the design phase. He therefore becomes involved early to define audit requirements, assess security standards, recommend needed controls, and review conversion tests. Knowledge of the application design is used to plan an audit guide for the installed EDP application."

2. Amount of EDP Competence of the Auditor

   The audit department has two potential sources of manpower which they are considering:

   1. Accountants - with a strong audit background and minor training in EDP.

   2. EDP Trained Personnel - with a strong background in all phases of data processing and systems analysis, but with only a minor audit background.

   The EDP trained individuals have more EDP technical competence while the accountants have greater schooling in auditing.

3. Assignment of Auditors to EDP Tasks

   Two alternatives are considered:

   1. Assignment of same personnel to both the design phase and subsequent operations phase audits. The department may prefer this because of efficiencies due to familiarity with the system.

   2. Assignment of different audit personnel to operations phase audit than those who participated during the design phase.

4. Internal Audit Organizational Relationships

An abstract of the organization chart of our hypothetical companies follows:

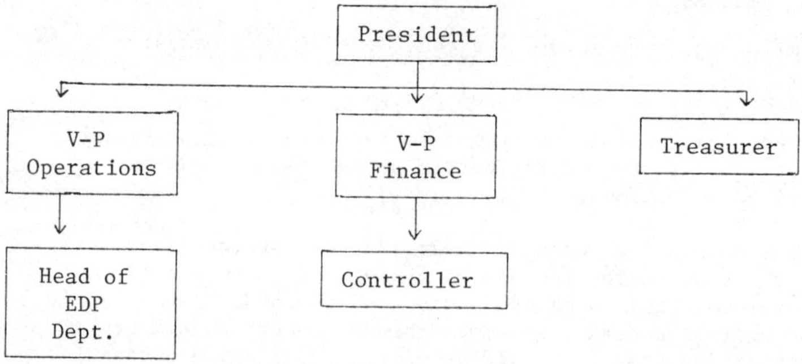

We are interested in knowing whether your perception of internal audit independence is affected by whether the internal audit departments reports to the Controller or the Vice-President of Finance.

CASES:

You will now be presented with 7 case situations. Please use your experience and knowledge of EDP auditing to rate the likelihood of an independent audit of EDP Application Controls during the operations phase. In order to focus on the four items described above, you may assume the auditor has a high degree of personal integrity and honesty.

You should indicate your rating in each case by circling the appropriate scale 1 to 5. The response categories are:

1. Not Independent
2. Unlikely to be Independent
3. Cannot Say
4. Likely to be Independent
5. Independent

In order for you to become familiar with this rating task, the first case is for practice.

PRACTICE CASE

The internal audit department participates in reviewing controls during the design phase of an EDP application. The work during the design phase and the subsequent application control audit is conducted by the same person who has extensive training and background in the EDP area. The internal audit department functionally reports to the Controller.

Likelihood of an Independent

Normal Audit of EDP Application Controls

1	2	3	4	5
Not Independent	Unlikely	Cannot Say	Likely	Independent

PLEASE TURN TO THE SET OF CASES ENTITLED:

<u>NORMAL AUDIT OF EDP APPLICATION CONTROLS</u>

TO RECORD YOUR RESPONSES

CASE SITUATIONS: COMPREHENSIVE POST AUDIT

The Comprehensive Post Audit

The comprehensive post audit is performed during the operations phase of a new computer development. In contrast to the control orientation of the normal audit of EDP application controls, this audit emphasizes the accomplishments of newly implemented computer applications. The auditor is concerned with such things as: 1) level of user satisfaction; 2) comparison of actual and estimated design cost; and 3) weakness in EDP development procedures. The objective is to critically analyze new computer applications and provide feedback which might improve the planning and control of future EDP development activities. The audit will generally include the following procedures:

1. Interviews with users

2. A comparison of reasons advanced for developing the EDP application with obtained results

3. A comparison of actual development cost with estimated cost

4. A review of development procedures and documentation

Factors to be Assessed:

The factors in the next set of cases are the same as in the first set except for the nature of the auditor's participation during the design phase of the application development.

1. Participation during design phase

   Two alternatives are considered:

   Level 1: Review emphasizing adherence to established procedures

   > "The auditor reviews the design activities and reports to management on the compliance of activities with company policies. For example, the auditor will ascertain whether competitive bids were taken for equipment, or if adequate security plans have been made. The auditor reviews controls and makes control recommendations. Periodic reports are issued at the completion of major stages of the design process."

Level 2: Project Assessment Orientation

"At this level of involvement the auditor becomes involved with the development process during the feasibility study, and remains involved during the remainder of the design process. His reporting responsibilities include:

1. Control recommendations, for both project development and application operation.

2. Adherence to company policies regarding EDP development procedures.

3. Reasonableness of time and cost estimates.

4. Assessment of appropriateness of the application and compatibility with present equipment.

The auditor reviews all system documentation, and may act as a liason between users and designers. There is a responsibility to sign an approval document at the completion of each major phase noting approval or deficiencies. Reported deficiencies will usually be supplemented with recommendations."

You will now be presented with 10 case situations in which you are to assess the likelihood that an independent comprehensive post audit (described above) will take place. The rating scale used is the same as with the first set of cases. You should indicate your rating in each case by circling the appropriate number.

PLEASE TURN TO THE SET OF CASES ENTITLED

COMPREHENSIVE POST AUDIT

TO RECORD YOUR RESPONSES

Now that you have completed your ratings of the 10 comprehensive post audit cases, please allocate 100 points to the 4 items in such a way as to indicate the relative importance of each item in assessing the likelihood of an independent comprehensive post audit. The more important items should be assigned more points than the less important items, and the total points should equal 100.

Item	Points
Level of Design Participation	_____
Assignment of Auditors	_____
Amount of EDP Background of Auditors	_____
Organizational Reporting Level of Internal Audit Department	_____
	100

1. Do you think auditors should perform the comprehensive post audit described on page 9?

   _____ Yes

   _____ No

   _____ Don't know

2. What level of involvement do you feel the auditor should participate during the design phase of an EDP application?

   _____ Auditor should not participate during design phase.

   _____ Level described in first set of cases, page 6.

   _____ Level 1, page 9

   _____ Level 2, page 10

3. The following is a list of audit activities that might be performed by an internal audit or EDP audit group during the design phase of a new EDP application. We are interested in knowing whether the performance of any of the activities listed below would affect your view of the auditor's independence when conducting an audit of the installed application. A negative response indicates your view that performance of the activity decreases the auditor's independence in performing subsequent work. If you give any activity a negative response, please indicate with a check mark in the *** column if you believe the possible negative impact of the activity would be offset or neutralized if the audit department had a policy of assigning different auditors to audits of the installed system than those who participated during the design phase.

	Effect on Your View of Independence			
Activity	Don't Know	None	Neg.	If negative, ***
a. Review design activities to assess adherence to company policies.	____	____	____	____
b. Recommend controls to be installed	____	____	____	____
c. Assist in design of needed processing controls	____	____	____	____
d. Review EDP application feasibility study for reasonableness, compatibility with present facilities; and report to management.	____	____	____	____
e. Act as a liason between programmers, users, and system design personnel	____	____	____	____
f. Specify audit trail and control requirements	____	____	____	____
g. Sign off at end of each major design phase noting approval or specifying deficiencies	____	____	____	____
h. Assess potential risks of proposed EDP application; report risks to management	____	____	____	____
i. Report on reasonableness of time and cost estimates	____	____	____	____
j. Other________________________________ ________________________________	____	____	____	____

4. OTHER FACTORS

Below is a list of factors that may, or may not affect your view of the ability of an internal audit department to conduct independent audits in the EDP area. The first four factors are those assessed in the case situations. Some of the factors are specifically related to audits in the EDP area while others are more descriptive of the general environment in which internal auditing functions. Please assess the importance of the possible effect of each factor on the independence of internal auditors conducting examinations in the EDP area. Some effects may be negative while others may have positive effects.

Example - The first item (a) is the extent that auditors are involved during the design phase of an EDP application. If this factor is <u>extremely important</u> you should give it a rating of 8 - 10. If it is not important rate it between 1 and 3. If it is <u>moderately important</u> rate it 4 - 7. The next factor (b) is assignment of personnel to different phases of audits. This may have an opposite effect from item (a). If it more than offsets the effect of (a) it should be rated higher in importance. If it doesn't it should be rated lower, but according to your estimate of overall importance. Other factors may not be as directly related as the first two, but their relative importance should be assessed in relation to previous answers. You may want to work through the items with a pencil before recording your final responses.

Factors Affecting

Internal Audit Independence

	Factor	Importance Low High
a.	Level of <u>participation</u> in design phase activities	1 2 3 4 5 6 7 8 9 10
b.	<u>Assignment of auditors</u> to different phases of the audit, e.g., pre-installation vs. post-installation.	1 2 3 4 5 6 7 8 9 10
c.	Amount of EDP background of the auditor, especially technical <u>EDP competence</u> of the auditor	1 2 3 4 5 6 7 8 9 10

4. Continued . . .

Factor	Importance Low ... High
d. Level in organization to which the head of internal auditing reports	1 2 3 4 5 6 7 8 9 10
e. Personal characteristics of the auditor	1 2 3 4 5 6 7 8 9 10
f. Evaluation methods by which auditors are reviewed for promotion	1 2 3 4 5 6 7 8 9 10
g. Staff Turnover, i.e., whether the audit department is viewed as a career position, or as training for other management positions	1 2 3 4 5 6 7 8 9 10
h. Project Composition; whether projects are staffed by a team of auditors, or by individual staff members	1 2 3 4 5 6 7 8 9 10
i. Responsibility Assumed by having auditor sign off at the end of major EDP application design phases noting his approval or reporting deficiencies	1 2 3 4 5 6 7 8 9 10
j. Code of Professional Ethics to which the internal auditor subscribes	1 2 3 4 5 6 7 8 9 10
k. Time Restrictions set on a job	1 2 3 4 5 6 7 8 9 10
l. Formality of Reports; whether all major findings are included in a formal report or are communicated informally	1 2 3 4 5 6 7 8 9 10
m. Top Management Support of internal audit department	1 2 3 4 5 6 7 8 9 10
n. Supervision and review of work papers by audit managers	1 2 3 4 5 6 7 8 9 10
o. Other ______________________ ______________________	1 2 3 4 5 6 7 8 9 10

5. For the 3 most important items rated above, would you briefly describe why you thought they were important?

Item 1:

Item 2:

Item 3:

6. Are there any additional EDP related activities in your organization that you believe would benefit by more review by the internal audit or EDP audit function?

Please make any additional comments on EDP auditing and internal audit independence that may be pertinent to this research.

THANK YOU. THE QUESTIONNAIRE IS NOW COMPLETE.

APPENDIX B

Characteristics of Companies Participating in the Study

List of Companies Participating in the Study

1. Aetna Life and Casualty Co., Hartford, CT
2. American National Bank & Trust Co., St. Paul
3. Burlington Northern Inc., St. Paul
4. CNA Financial Corp., Chicago
5. Chemical Bank, New York
6. Chrysler Corp., Detroit
7. Continental Illinois National Bank & Trust Co. of Chicago
8. Control Data Corp., Minneapolis
9. Dart Industries Inc., Los Angeles
10. Dayton-Hudson Corp., Minneapolis
11. Farmers and Mechanics Savings Bank, Minneapolis
12. Finance America Corp., Allentown, PA
13. First Computer Corp., St. Paul
14. First National City Bank, Chicago
15. General Mills Inc., Minneapolis
16. Green Giant Co., LeSueur, MN
17. Harris Trust and Savings Bank, Chicago
18. Hartford Insurance Group, Hartford
19. Honeywell Inc., Minneapolis
20. Hughes Aircraft Co., Los Angeles
21. Investors Diversified Services Inc., Minneapolis
22. Kraftco Corp., Glenview, IL
23. Land O' Lakes Inc., Minneapolis
24. Manufacturers Hanover Trust Co., New York
25. Massachusetts Mutual Life Insurance Co., Springfield, MA
26. Minnesota Mining and Manufacturing, St. Paul
27. Minnesota Mutual Life Insurance Co., St. Paul
28. Montgomery Ward & Co., Chicago
29. National Car Rental System Inc., Minneapolis
30. Northern States Power Co., Minneapolis
31. Northwest Bancorporation, Minneapolis
32. Northwestern National Life Insurance Co., Minneapolis
33. Pacific Gas and Electric Co., San Francisco
34. Quaker Oats Co., Chicago
35. Rockwell International Corp., Pittsburgh
36. St. Paul Companies Inc., St. Paul
37. United States Steel Corp., Pittsburgh
38. Wells Fargo Bank, National Association, San Francisco
39. Western Southern Life Insurance Co., Cincinnati
40. Xerox Corp., Rochester, NY
41. One large company requested that its name not be mentioned.

Table 18
Sample Companies' Lines of Business

Line of Business	Number	Percent
Manufacturing	15	37%
Banking	10	24%
Insurance and other financial	10	24%
Utilities	2	5%
Retail	2	5%
Transportation	2	5%
Total	41	100%

The companies participating in the study represent diverse lines of business. Banking and other financial institutions represent about 50% of the sample population and manufacturing represents 33%.

Table 19
Size and Existence of EDP Audit Function

Number of Years the Internal Audit Department Has Had One or More Individuals Devoting Full Time to EDP Auditing	Number	Percent
1 year or less	14	34%
2-3 years	7	17%
4-5 years	9	22%
6 or more years	11	27%
Total	41	100%
Existence of Separate EDP Audit Section		
Separate EDP audit section	29	71%
No EDP audit section but doing some EDP auditing	12	29%
Total	41	100%
Size of EDP Audit Department		
1 staff member	5	17%
2-4 members	7	24%
5 or more staff members	17	59%
Total	29	100%

Table 19 shows the diversity in the size and existence of an EDP audit function. Slightly over two-thirds of the companies had a separate EDP audit section. While many of the companies had relatively little EDP audit experience, 26% had over six years of EDP audit experience, whereas another 21% had between four and five years. Most of the companies with a separate EDP audit section had experienced rapid growth, and approximately 60% of those companies had an EDP staff in excess of five individuals.

Table 20
Size of EDP Systems Measured by Monthly Equipment and Software Rental*

Monthly Equipment and Software Rental	Number of Companies	Percentage
Under $50,000	3	11%
$50,000 - $100,000	5	18%
$100,000 - $200,000	4	14%
$200,000 - $300,000	1	4%
Over $300,000	15	54%
Total	28	100%

* Based on responses from 28 questionnaires returned from data processing personnel. A review of the companies that did not return the EDP Department questionnaire, but returned other questionnaires included in the study, led to the conclusion that the computer systems in these other companies were at least as large and complex as those described in tables 20 and 21.

Table 21
EDP Department Heads' Rating of EDP System Complexity**

Complexity Rating	Number	Percentage
Low 1	0	0%
2	1	3%
3	3	11%
4	12	43%
High 5	12	43%
Total	28	100%
Mean Response	4.32	

** The complexity rating was described in the questionnaire as follows: "A rating of 1 indicates a relatively simple batch processing system; a rating of 5 indicates a highly complex, interrelated system in which an audit trail is not easily followed."

Table 22
Distribution of EDP Audit Time

Audit Area	Percent of Audit Time Devoted to Area*
Design phase	23%
Existing EDP applications	33%
EDP facility organization and processing efficiency	18%
Support services for management and other audit personnel	17%
Other	9%
Total	100%

* Represents the mean of 36 responses from EDP audit managers.

Both design-phase and postinstallation audits are important to the companies participating in the study. Table 22 shows the average distribution of EDP audit time the sample companies devoted to major EDP audit areas. Although some companies are not involved with design-phase audits, an average of 23% of EDP audit time in the sampled companies is devoted to the design phase.

Table 23
Percentage of EDP Audit Time Devoted to Design-Phase Audit Activities

Percentage of Total EDP Audit Time Spent on Design Phase	Number of Companies Within Category	Percentage of Companies Within Category
0-5%	8	21%
6-19%	12	31%
20-30%	11	28%
40% and over	8	21%
Total	39	100%

The companies differ considerably in the performance of design-phase auditing, as seen above. Approximately 20% of the companies spent virtually no EDP audit time on design-phase audit activities, whereas another 20% spent almost half of their EDP audit time during the design phase.